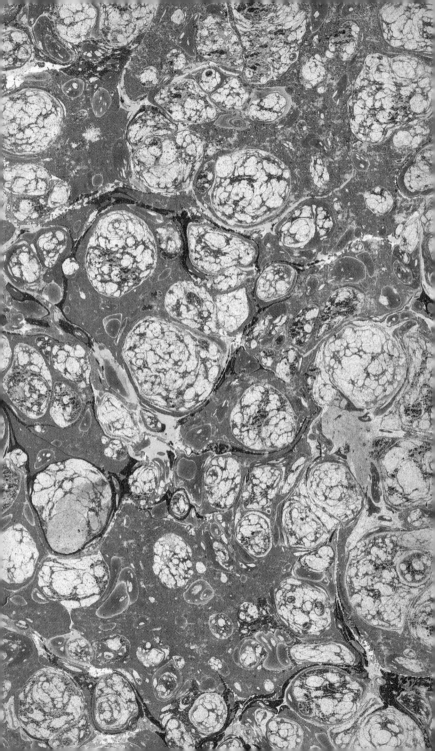

A VOYAGE
TO
AUSTRALIA

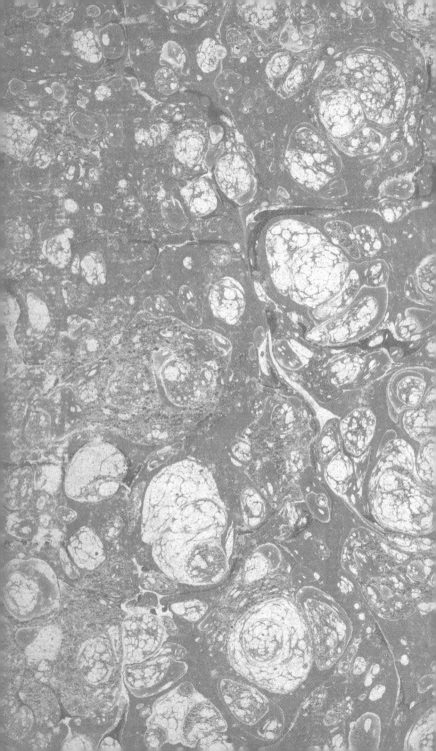

Private Journal of

A VOYAGE
TO
AUSTRALIA
1838–39

James Bell

Edited by Richard Walsh, with an introduction and
epilogue by Anthony Laube

ALLEN&UNWIN

First published in 2011

Copyright in this volume © Allen & Unwin Pty Ltd 2011

The Publisher would like to acknowledge the State Library of South Australia as the owner of the original document *Private Journal of a Voyage to Australia, 1838–39* by James Bell, which was purchased with funds from the State Library of South Australia Foundation and which remains the property of and in the possession of the State Library.

Allen & Unwin
Sydney, Melbourne, Auckland, London

83 Alexander Street
Crows Nest NSW 2065
Australia
Phone: (61 2) 8425 0100
Fax: (61 2) 9906 2218
Email: info@allenandunwin.com
Web: www.allenandunwin.com

Cataloguing-in-Publication details are available
from the National Library of Australia
www.trove.nla.gov.au

ISBN 978 1 74237 795 7

Internal design by Lisa White
Set in 11/16 pt Minion Pro and Didot LT Std by Bookhouse, Sydney
Printed in China by Everbest Printing Co Ltd

10 9 8 7 6 5 4 3 2 1

CONTENTS

James Bell
1838

A NOTE TO THE READER

This is not a wholly accurate transcription of James Bell's handwritten journal. He was a poor and inconsistent speller; he often wrote under very unfavourable conditions, sitting on a rolling deck while presumably balancing his ink pot and dip pen. The original manuscript contains obvious omissions and other carelessnesses that would exhaust readers if they were transcribed faithfully. There are instances where his scrawl defies deciphering.

I have tried to maintain the improvisation and spontaneity of the original text, but to balance that against a need for ease of reading. Inconsistency in his spelling is very confusing, so it has mainly been eliminated, as have some of the abbreviated forms of words he customarily uses in his haste to put nib to paper. His capitalisation too is very inconsistent, but this has mainly been retained so as to give readers the flavour of the original text.

At times I have convinced myself that I could read what seems virtually indecipherable; at other times I have simply guessed. It seems too much of an impediment to reader enjoyment for there to be words missing.

I have taken great liberties with his punctuation. It is not one of his fortes and it seems important for the modern reader to readily grasp what he intends. I have very occasionally made the kind of change to the text that I would have urged upon him if he were alive today and wanting to communicate readily with his readers. While the authenticity of obscurity and meaninglessness may have some proponents, I am not of their number.

James Bell was a lover of poetry and he quoted many of his favourite passages in his journal. He had some of his favourite books with him and no doubt attempted to copy them accurately. At other times he was probably falling back on his unreliable memory. To enable the modern reader to share Bell's delight in this verse, I have at all times used each poet's original text rather than Bell's imperfect renditions.

Sustained by his sense of adventure, his love of poetry, his faith in his Presbyterian God and his fond memories of old friends and particularly the mysterious 'C.P.', James Bell maintained a lively and astute record of his historic journey. This text, as edited, is intended to allow his voice to be heard vividly more than a century and a half later.

RICHARD WALSH

INTRODUCTION

BY ANTHONY LAUBE

On 16 May 1839, the barque *Planter* finally made its way into the Port River, and along to the rough wharves and slab buildings which made up the makeshift port of the young city of Adelaide. For James Bell and his fellow passengers, the journey had been long and eventful. Each of the 120 adults and children on board had looked forward to this day, this arrival at last at the not quite two-year-old capital among the gum trees, in Her Majesty's newest colony, South Australia.

Adelaide had been laid out in 1837, by Colonel William Light, at the direction of the South Australian Colonization Commissioners. The king, William IV, had stipulated the 'chief town' of the new colony should be named after his wife. The Colonization Commissioners required simply that Light site the city within a workable distance of a safe port, with access to both drinkable water and arable land. With the city's first residents camping on the beach at Glenelg waiting for his decision, Light, under pressure, chose a site on the broad plain of Tandanya ('the red kangaroo'), between the hills and the sea, with the River Torrens running through it, several controversial kilometres inland from his chosen port.

From its very beginnings, one of South Australia's attractions for British immigrants was the banning of convict labour—although the first settlers must have recognised the irony that the author of South Australia's colonisation plan was himself in jail. Edward Gibbon Wakefield had developed his theories about the renewal of the British population through colonisation abroad while he was serving time for a personal get-rich scheme, which had involved the abduction of a teenage heiress. In Newgate Prison he had met returned convicts from New South Wales, whose tales of Australia's opportunities inspired him to apply his theories to the land down under. Many from the British middle classes were looking for escape from social, religious and legal restrictions. Wakefield's great achievement via his writings was to bring the middle classes to view immigration as a potentially respectable pursuit and not merely the domain of convicts and other roughnecks.

In 1830 the explorer Charles Sturt had followed the course of the mighty River Murray down into unexplored South Australia, thus putting this region on the map and bringing it into the consciousness of the English reading public. With a group of fellow idealists, young Robert Gouger—who, like Wakefield, was looking to raise funds to get married, but intended to do so within the law—took up Wakefield's plan and Sturt's discovery. Meetings were held and Parliament lobbied until the aged Duke of Wellington lent his support for the passing of the South Australian Act in 1834. This established a board of ten Colonization Commissioners under the leadership of Colonel Robert Torrens, charged to make the theory a reality.

The essence of Wakefield's plan, publicised and firmed into practical detail with input from many, including Gouger, was for land in the new colony to be sold (rather than given away) so that the money raised could be used to fund immigration of respectable labourers. The Commissioners were given the twin tasks of finding middle-class adventurers prepared to buy land in distant South Australia, and selecting respectable labourers to work it.

Torrens bombarded the public with an amazing media campaign, which saw the publishing of 20 books and 40 pamphlets about South Australia. A newspaper, the *South Australian Colonist*, further extolled the idyllic colony-to-be. Torrens travelled throughout England, Scotland and Ireland, giving lectures and commissioning a series of 'emigration agents' to enlist suitable labourers; thirteen agents in England, four in Scotland and one in Ireland set to recruiting. Applicants needed to fall within 25 stipulated occupational groups, and be aged between fifteen and 30; they required testimonials from ministers, doctors and neighbours. An additional precaution was the promise of a payment to the agents of £1 for each assisted immigrant landed in

South Australia with a record of good behaviour while at sea.[1] Of the flurry of 9000 applications forwarded to the Commissioners in the first four years, 4000 were rejected.[2]

Middle-class cash settlers were attracted by the promise of a convict-free, fertile land, and an escape from many of the restrictions of home. It was the ambitious who were both targeted and attracted by the scheme. Many pious men and women—perhaps including James Bell—were also lured by the promise of freedom from the dominance of a state religion. Torrens' campaigning attracted a large number of former military men on limited incomes, as well as canny tradesmen seeing the opportunity to set up businesses in a newly founded city. A surprising number of widows and widowers seemed to see the colony as a remarriage bureau. And, as always, once the first settlers made their decision, friends, neighbours and a variety of relations followed them. An important lure for the paying immigrants was that every £20 spent on land purchases permitted nomination of one servant or favoured labourer to accompany their masters on a free ticket.

Determined to see the plan go ahead for the sake of religious freedom, a rich Baptist, George Fife Angas, resigned as a Colonization Commissioner to float an investment portfolio—the South Australian Company. In doing so,

---

1 Douglas Pike, *Paradise of Dissent*, Longmans Green & Co., London, 1957, p. 151.
2 Ibid.

Angas singlehandedly saved the whole scheme from floundering when it looked like being short of raising the £115,000 which Parliament demanded the Commissioners must have in hand before any ships set sail. Purchasing large tracts of land in South Australia at a special rate, Angas nominated 350 labourers, even buying his own ships to transport the travellers.

The Commissioners took careful steps to ensure safe travel for the founding families of their ideal settlement. A year before the first ships set out, in 1835, the Passenger Act was passed, restricting passenger numbers according to ship size. The Act also set minimum water and food rations, and sleeping accommodation guidelines. The Commissioners established a Shipping Committee, which was vigilant in procuring the best ships on offer, regardless of additional cost. The *Planter* was just three years old when commissioned for her trip to South Australia. An important incentive was that the owners of vessels received only half their commission up front—the balance being payable based on a favourable report at the completion of the journey.

James Bell's countryman James Horsburgh published his first guidebook to sea routes in 1809. With updated editions, this remained the standard text for decades. For sailing ships, with only the wind and currents for propulsion, the usual course was to allow the north-east trade winds and natural drift to carry vessels in a diagonal direction southwards towards South America, passing through the dreaded equatorial doldrums. From the South American coast the course was then south-easterly towards Africa, and then south again, hopefully into the 'roaring forties' where both wind and current would make for a quick trip across the Indian Ocean to Australia. Ideally, the trip would be completed without the difficulties of calling into foreign ports en route. But in reality the depletion of supplies—especially that most precious commodity, fresh water—meant calling in at Rio de Janeiro or some of the islands on the way. The Cape of Good Hope, at the tip of Africa, was a port of last resort due to its problematic harbour—easy enough to enter, more difficult to get clear of. A passage of less than 100 days from London to South Australia was a very good one—but invariably the trip took weeks longer, averaging closer to 130 days.

Captains planned for a return trip minus passengers. On arriving in the young colony, several weeks were spent gathering cargo and supplies—advertising in Adelaide's two newspapers—before travelling on to the older Australian colonies, then on through Java and the Chinese ports back to London. Shipping agents were among the first business speculators in Adelaide, often simply extending the businesses they had already established in the other colonies. Brothers Emanuel and Vaiben Solomon of Sydney were perhaps the first shipping agents in South Australia, along with their Hebraic brothers, the Montefiores—relatives of Colonization Commissioner Jacob Montefiore. These agents stockpiled goods in readiness to broker a good deal with returning ships.

Three classes of travel were offered to the prospective immigrant. 'Cabin' passengers were the business class of the day. Paying around £65 each for a cabin on the quarterdeck, usually a little over three by three metres in size, they took their meals with the captain, had fresh meat daily with a pint of wine *and* helpings of spirits and malt liquor. Quantities and types of food and drink for the three classes were carefully set out in a table compiled by the Commissioners. Most travellers recorded being well fed.

Intermediate passengers, such as James Bell, paid around half the amount—about £30 each—for a cabin below deck. This was an agricultural labourer's total annual wages in South Australia in 1838. The intermediate cabins were smaller, at two by two metres, arranged on either side of a communal meeting space. With only slightly less varied meals than the cabin passengers received, including a lesser consignment of alcohol (one bottle of wine per week), they were served by either a designated cook/servant—as seems to have been the case on the *Planter* with its small number of intermediate passengers—or by an elected 'mess captain', who drew the rations for six or eight passengers, taking the food to the galley to be cooked before serving.[3]

A partition separated the intermediate few from the steerage many. Steerage was not unlike a large dormitory, with curtained cabins containing double-tiered bunks.

---

3   Colin Kerr, *A Excelent Coliney: The practical idealists of 1836–1846*, Rigby, Adelaide, 1978, pp. 19–20.

Family cabins separated the single men in single bunks from the single women in shared bunks. Along the centre of the steerage accommodation ran a long fixed table and benches. Steerage menus were not as varied as those of the other two classes, but steerage travellers were allowed half a gill (around 70 millilitres) of rum per day.

For each vessel the Commissioners hired a doctor. The *Planter*'s Samuel Harris was to receive seven shillings per passenger landed safely in South Australia—always provided that when passengers were examined by the South Australian Emigration Agent at the end of the journey he was found to have carried out his duties faithfully. His total fee would have been around £50. To assist him, the Commissioners appointed a Presbyterian minister turned schoolteacher, James Macgowan, who was taking his large family to Adelaide. Satisfactory performance on the surgeon assistant's part would entitle him to a not inconsiderable payment of one-third of the doctor's salary. Both positions were according to standard procedures set down for all vessels chartered by the Commissioners.[4]

Among themselves, travellers often appointed two or three 'constables' under a head constable—the latter being paid £5. And from 1839 the Commissioners also appointed a schoolteacher to each vessel. Although the *Planter* did not

---

4 Colonization Commissioners for South Australia, letterbook, copies of letters to the resident commissioner 1836–40 (State Records of South Australia GRG 48/5/1), p. 222.

have a teacher appointed by the Commissioners, it did have elected constables.

Apart from the human passengers, stock, mostly destined for the menu, was housed on deck. Passing through the tropics, passengers of all classes might sleep on deck with the animals for the sake of avoiding stifling, smelly cabins below deck, as becalmed vessels crept their way down the vast ocean stretches towards Australia.

This, then, was the scene for 120 travellers leaving the shores of Britain in the winter of 1838, seeking a new life in youthful, utopian Adelaide. Risking their savings on a potentially hazardous voyage, or having passed the stringent guidelines set by Parliament and the Commissioners for a free ticket, all of them set forth hoping the *Planter* would carry them towards the realisation of their dreams for advancement, and maybe even love, on the other side of the globe. For young James Bell, the *Planter* carried him towards the hope of a new home which might soon be shared with loved ones for now left behind.

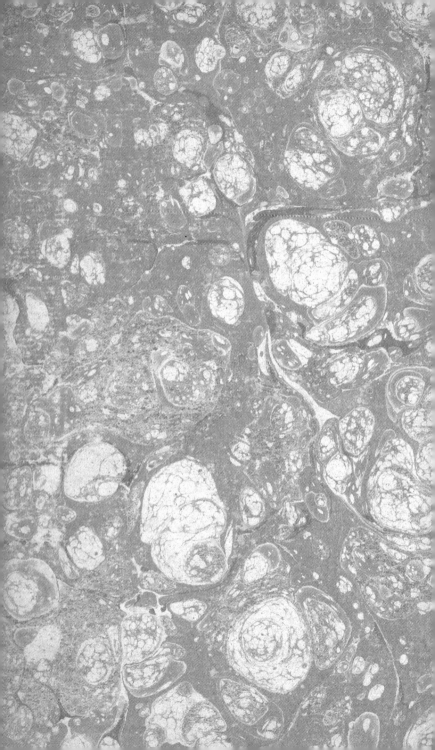

Private Journal of

A VOYAGE
TO
AUSTRALIA

1838–39

James Bell

Private

Journal

of

A Voyage to Australia

1838-39-

By.

James Bell

Ben
Bass

Kept in conformity with a promise
made t. C. Perry Bellisle St. Working
and with the intention of being sent to
her, as a small token of respect for the
many good qualities and the friendship
with which she has honored me —

Kept in conformity with a promise made to
C. Perry, Bellisle St* Workington, and with the
intention of being sent to her, as a small token
of respect for her many good qualities and the
friendship with which she has honored me—

James Bell, 1838

---

* This appears clearly in more than one place in the 1841 British Census as 'Bell Isle Street'.

Preface

The following is not merely an account
of the Ships course, and a mere mention of
the places passed during my voyage to South
Australia, but a noting down from day
to day of the thoughts and ideas that
occupied my mind at the moment — and my
reason for this was, that I might bring
my observation of events as well as manners
to bear more directly upon my own conduct
& in this way correct any thing that
might be amiss, as well as tending to
the strengthening of those principles with
which my mind has been imbued — as
I am convinced that this is the best way
of fixing occurrences upon the memory —
consequently it is to be considered wholly
private. This will account for any
mention of my own affairs in such a
way as does not usually occur in a journal
and the Friend to whom I may send it
will understand this — and that it may
never be read by a third Party —

Preface

The following is not merely an account of the Ships course, and a mere mention of the places passed during my voyage to South Australia, but a noting down from day to day of the thoughts and ideas that occupied my mind at the moment—and my reason for this was that I might bring my observation of events, as well as manners, to bear more directly upon my own conduct, & in this way correct any thing that might be amiss, as well as tending to the strengthening of those principles with which my mind has been imbued, as I am convinced that this is the best way of fixing occurrences upon the memory. Consequently, it is to be considered wholly private. This will account for any mention of my own affairs in such a way as does not usually occur in a journal and the Friend to whom I may send it will understand this—and that it must never be read by a third party.

—J.B.

1838

25 Nov: 1838. Sunday — sailed at 5
O'clock A.M. from Deptford in the
Planter — Capt. Beazley — She left
St. Kathrines Dock London on Monday
but has been delayed till this morning
at Deptford, and this is an instance
of the vexatious delays occasioned to
passengers by the unaccountable con.
of Capts. & Owners of such Vessels —

We have on board a number
poor people with their families, who
induced by poverty at home and a
belief that there is more of this worlds
goods to be acquired in the far distant
colony of S. Australia — have clung to it
as a last hope — who knows what
fancies they indulge, perhaps they
think of becoming rich. may I
so, as a reward of their adventurous
Spirit, and may God keep from
them all disease until that he at
restores them to the open air, and the
accustomed mode of living —

We are being towed by a Steam
and have passed Gravesend and shall

25 November 1838. Sunday

Sailed at 5 oClock a.m. from Deptford in the Ship
'Planter' under Capt Beazley.* She left the St Kathrines
Dock† London on Monday, but has been delayed till
this morning at Deptford‡, and this is an instance
of the vexatious delays occasioned to passengers by
the unaccountable conduct of Capts & Owners of
such Vessels.

We have on board a number of poor people with
their families who, induced by poverty at home and

---

* The *Planter* was a 347-ton ship built at Newcastle on Tyne
  in 1835. Its captain was Thomas Beazley. According to the
  Manifests of Vessels Arriving from Overseas 1838–42 in the
  South Australian Archives, it carried 106 passengers to South
  Australia.
† St Katharine Docks, as is the usual spelling, were officially
  opened on 25 October 1828 and situated on the north bank
  of the Thames, downstream of the Tower of London. This is
  now the Docklands.
‡ Deptford Wharf was about ten miles downstream. Deptford
  Dockyard had been created in 1513 by Henry VIII to provide
  boats for the Royal Navy.

a belief that there is more of this worlds goods to be acquired in the far distant colony of S. Australia, have clung to it as a last hope. Who knows what fancies they indulge—perhaps they think of becoming rich. May it be so, as a reward of their adventurous spirit, and may God keep from them all disease until that he again restores them to the open air, and their accustomed mode of living. We are being towed by a Steamer and have passed Gravesend and shall soon lose sight of Britain, & steer our course into the great Ocean and trust ourselves to the protection of God.

The Steerage passengers are sent out by the Colonization Commissioners*—and are a motley group. There is a surgeon†, a young man to whom I have been introduced—I think that his experience of his profession cannot be great, and I shall be happy if our Voyage does not add to it.

We have passed a great number of Vessels of all sizes; carrying the produce of every clime to London, that mart for the merchandise of the whole world. They appear most beautiful this calm evening, with all sail set and bearing up with the tide.

---

* The South Australian Colonization Commission was gazetted in May 1835. In January 1836, four ships sailed from England on behalf of the South Australian Company. They developed a settlement on Kangaroo Island in July 1836 but, when farming proved unviable there, transferred to the mainland.

† The surgeon's name was Samuel Harris.

We now turn southward and, still towed onward, we pass the fixed lights placed to direct the nightly mariner on his watery way. Anchored about 6 oClock in the evening and, as our Pilot dreads a squall, we make all secure.

26 November 1838. Monday

It blows fresh and straight in our face so we cannot stir. I am a little sick this morning, and vomit a little. It continues to blow, and my sickness increases.

27 November 1838. Tuesday

Still blows a stiff breeze, and we are fixed in our place, which is rather a dangerous one, among sands. Our Capt thinks of slipping his cable if the gale increases, and running before the wind to reach a place of safety. This is rather dangerous among sands and this, added to my sickness, makes me rather low spirited. Night sets in and, while the sea runs very high, we wish for morning.

I go to sleep and dream of friends far distant. Morning at length arrives—the wind is calmer and south west.

28 November 1838. Wednesday

After last nights hurricane we have a calmer wind and more favourable. The anchor is up and our sails set. By tacking to and fro we move on.

My sickness has disappeared to day and I feel renovated spirits, and I trust shall feel no more of it. I am up betimes and beat about—to keep myself in exercise.

2 p.m. The wind again increases and we are again forced to furl the sails and let go the anchor as we cannot get round the foreland. It increases to a perfect hurricane, and our Vessel labours exceedingly. I feel my sickness again returning and go to bed.

We let out all the cable and have the second anchor ready in case of need. I spend a rather anxious night &, unused as I am to gales of wind, I think there is little pleasure in it.

29 November 1838. Thursday

Dreadful hurricane. We continue at anchor rocked about fearfully and expect to be driven from our anchorage every moment. I think this no good beginning of my voyage. But I have trust in that God who alone can protect me, and I do not feel fear. It blows all day.

A Voyage to Australia

The decks are covered with spray and here we are surrounded by sand banks, and in the midst of danger. A boat & 6 men cased in oilcloth, with the waves going over them every instant, pass us. I am told that they are going round to report to Loyds[*] in what position the Vessels are lying. My friend Johnstone will not think much of his risk in the 'Planter' this evening[†]—however, he may be anxious for my safety. We will be reported all safe, but who knows how long.

It is vexatious that we have been at sea since Sunday morning & have only got such a little way on our voyage. As the Sailors say a 'bad beginning makes a good ending'. I hope it will be so in my experience. A Dublin Steamer[‡] has passed us. She

---

[*] The great insurance house, Lloyd's of London, had started in around 1688 in Edward Lloyd's coffee house in Tower Street, London.

[†] The cargo manifest includes goods for 'H. Johnstone'. There were Johnston brothers in South Australia—William was a well-known spirit merchant; the other, John, a tailor in the city. John Johnston appears in the communicant list for Gouger Street Presbyterian Church, which Bell joined in Adelaide. There is no known connection with the 'H. Johnstone' of the cargo list and the brothers.

[‡] The first steamship credited with crossing the Atlantic Ocean was an American ship, the SS *Savannah*, in 1819, but she was actually a hybrid between a steamship and a sailing ship. Iron-hulled steamships first made the journey to Australia in 1852. However, these early steamers, known as auxiliaries,

weathers it bravely. I wish we could make as much progress.

I do not feel so sick to day and have an appetite. I am dreadfully annoyed by a shocking brute of a first mate, named *Mustart*, who is never right but when he is swearing about something. Altho he is very civil to me, I must call him a most accomplished Brute in his discourse. I am most uncomfortably annoyed with him.

The poor Steerage passengers are most uncomfortably situated, exposed to cold and treated with insolence. A few of them are respectable looking people tho' poor & there is a Clergyman.* I don't know what bad luck has placed him in his present position, but it makes my heart sicken to see him—his office treated with disrespect by men who certainly are, in comparison, but as the chaff to the wheat.

I have just overheard a quarrel between our Carpenter† & Mate, arising, as most quarrels do, out of nothing. The Capt is appealed to. The Villain of a Mate possesses the best *lingo* and a greater variety of oaths; he has, by implicating the Capt in the

---

    still carried a full set of sails, because of their inefficient engines and the lack of coaling ports en route.

* This was Reverend James Macgowan, a schoolmaster, of whom much more will be heard. In time James Bell was to revise his sympathy for this ill-fated gentleman.

† The ship's carpenter appears on the manifest as 'McDonald'.

Carpenters list of arguments to convince him of his error, set the Capt against the poor old Carpenter, whose only fault is that his temper is rather short—he is of grumbling disposition. I had not been impressed very favourably with the Carpenter, but I do not like to see him abused. The Capt expends a volley or two of oaths about the matter, so I suppose it is over—not much to the credit of the parties concerned—and does not increase my opinion of our Capt.

The wind is rather abated and I hope the gale is going to abate.

The gale increased during the evening.

30 November 1838. Friday

Spent a sleepless night owing to the highness of the wind. I thought every moment that we must have been driven from our anchorage. This morning it is calmer and we again endeavour to proceed a little—we reach Margate Roads* and there we cast anchor. I cant tell how long. The people are more lively to day and Sea

---

* After five days the *Planter* has reached the deep water anchorage known as Margate Roads, north of Margate in Kent and at the eastern end of the Thames Estuary. For incoming vessels this was a designated area for taking on pilots; it was a holding area for outgoing vessels awaiting their orders to proceed out of the estuary.

sickness seems to have done them no harm, unless an increase of appetite can be considered such.

1 December 1838. Saturday

The wind still unfavourable and we keep our anchorage—unable to make sail.

2 December 1838. Sunday

Wind still ahead of us. The Sabbath is not ushered in with devotion here—every thing goes on as on any other day and I think we shall soon forget when this sacred day comes round. We have some few Wesleyan Methodists aboard—they make a pretence of singing hymns and reading prayers, but such hypocrisy as they display is indeed most disgusting.

3 December 1838. Monday

After a most boisterous night it is calm this morning— and I hear them preparing for another attempt at passing the Foreland.*

---

* The North Foreland is a chalk headland on the eastern end of the Isle of Thanet, on the Kentish coast, and commands views over the southern North Sea. Fifteen kilometres south of it is another chalk headland called the South Foreland,

By dint of tacking backwards & forwards, we have succeeded and cast anchors in the Downs in safety. I don't know how long we may have to stay here waiting for a favourable wind—it blows straight from the south. I have written to C.P. & Brother Chas.* I have had a letter written for the former for several days, waiting for our arrival here to send it. I hear the Pilot saying that this has been the roughest voyage he ever performed between London and the Downs—but I suppose he will say the same of the next Vessel he conducts.

4 December 1838. Tuesday

Still in the Downs. Wind to day the same. It is rather calm, and it gives some pleasure to see the vessels moored along side and to look upon the shore.

I had a strange dream last night—I fancied myself at home among my friends & some of them too who I trust are now in heaven. In fact my thoughts run back to home and the joys I once possessed in the

---

which overlooks the Straits of Dover. Between these two landmarks lies the area of sea called the Downs.

* The 1841 Census lists a family at Lockerbie Street, Dryfesdale, Dumfriesshire, which includes an elderly couple, Thomas (probably James's uncle, whom he refers to later) and Margaret Bell; a Charles Bell, aged 28, 'road latonen' (*sic*); and Adam Bell, 25, same occupation; plus five-year-old Isabella Mundell.

company of dear friends, that I may well sing with
Goldsmith:

> *Where'er I roam, whatever realms to see,*
> *My heart, untravelled, fondly turns to thee:*
> *Still to my brother turns with ceaseless pain,*
> *And drags at each remove a lengthening chain.**

And with all my heart I can add:

> *Eternal blessings crown my earliest friends*
> *And round their dwellings guardian saints attend*
> *Blest be that spot—*†

If this were a proper place for the purpose, these
words seem in a remarkable manner to express my
feelings towards another object—and if this ever falls
into her hands, she will oblige me by making a slight
alteration in them so as to suit the purpose.

I have not gone ashore here—the Boatmen charge
10/. each way, so I think this is more than I ought
to pay for the pleasure. I never saw in any place
people with less compunction in regard to charges.
It is to be accounted for by the precarious nature of
their employments as they are many days without

---

* Oliver Goldsmith, *The Traveller* (1764).
† In the original poem, it is 'friend' and 'his dwelling'.

employment at a time. They are accordingly active in cases of shipwreck and have saved many valuable lives. But, strange to say, instead of being rewarded for risking their lives to save those of others, they are obliged to put up with any small pittance they may receive from private individuals interested, and that given almost in the way of charity. Why should there not be a fund here, as in some other places, for rewarding such persons in a manner proportioned to their services.

5 December 1838. Wednesday

Wind west. We set sail at 6 oClock and get on slowly. The coast of France bounds our view on the one hand and on the other we have the rugged coast of Kent. The Sea seems as if it was restrained from overflowing the country only by the immense precipice of chalk soil opposed to the waves.

We pass Dover. It presents a beautiful appearance. The town lying in a *niche* of the coast, presenting a low beach opposite the town and bounded on each hand by high banks, the view extending forward along the vale till lost in distance. The Castle situated above and overlooking the whole, while on each side the landscape embellished by a thousand smiling cottages. The bold and prominent outline of the coast, only interrupted as it were to afford a site for the town, all make the view truly romantic and delightful.

The distance to Calais is very short and steamboats ply across constantly. Dover castle commands both the town and the Sea and appears to be a strong barrier against an enemy landing on this part of the coast.* I have heard a vague report of 150 vessels having been lost along the English coast south of the Thames last week. I trust however it is false. I feel to day perfectly well, and trust that I shall continue so.

6 December 1838. Thursday

The fine breeze of yesterday, which gradually veered round to north west, has sunk this morning into a calm and we scarcely feel any motion. We have however got opposite the Isle of Wight† and the blue hills of Old England are now scarce visible above the horizon, our course being south west. The Sea is now of its proper blue and the sky clear, the air tho' chill is bracing. Capt Beazley is very attentive

---

* James Bell was born in the year after the Battle of Waterloo and the conclusion of the Napoleonic Wars. However, an Englishman—or indeed a Scotsman—in this era would continue to be conscious of the implications, in any future conflict, of the proximity of Calais to Dover.
† The Isle of Wight is five to eight kilometres off the Hampshire Coast, from which it is separated by the Solent.

to his duty and seems to take much pleasure in the ship's sailing fast.

Our Steerage Passengers have now had time to display the clovenfoot* instead of the assumed one, and I am sorry to say there are some among them with whom I must find fault—indeed I believe them to be of very bad character, and I think I may say as much of some in a more respectable part of the Ship. I shall mark† the seeming Gents who act so unbecomingly.

As to the wretched female Emigrants‡, I am only sorry that so fine a country as that to which they are going should be defiled by their footsteps—and wonder how the Comrs should think themselves free from blame in encouraging such, by affording them a free passage. In fact I think there are some ½ doz. of them of the Class called 'unfortunates'§—they are single women.

I have now got my habits conformed to my situation. I have my hours for writing, reading, walking, eating, sleeping—and continue in these ways to pass

---

* Traditionally, this is the sign of the Devil.

† Here 'mark' is probably being used in its older meaning—*to make a note of*.

‡ There were at least nine single women on the ship, some brought as servants to the wealthier passengers, together with three Durieu daughters and three Macgowan daughters, and other, younger teenage girls.

§ A euphemism for prostitutes.

my time. But 4 months will, I am afraid, exhaust all my reserves.

7 December 1838. Friday

About 8 oClock last night the breeze again sprang up, but was rather foul. It continued so till 12 to day, when it became again north west and pretty fresh. We had been tacking during the night and forenoon, but we now set more sail and the vessel darted off beautifully. The tide setting in from the Bay of Biscay prevented her from reaching her utmost speed, but we have made from 5 to 7 miles an hour. I cannot imagine a more splendid spectacle than a gallant barque* breasting the saucy wave, which lashes her sides in impotent rage and expends itself in foam while she careers onward in proud defiance of the surrounding waters.

At 4 p.m. they are looking out for the Portland point lighthouse.† I have finished reading Blacklock

---

* Any sailing ship can be described as a barque, but typically it has three masts, with the foremast and mainmast square-rigged and the mizzenmast rigged fore and aft.

† The Isle of Portland is a limestone peninsula jutting into the English Channel south of Weymouth in Dorset, to which it is connected by Chesil Beach.

on Sheep*—and other Publications as to Australia. Also Scott's Marmion and Lady of the Lake.†

8 December 1838. Saturday

Wind fair & calm. We make little progress—towards midday we are almost as 'idle as a painted Ship upon a painted ocean'.‡ We are out of sight of land & steer south west. I think my journal after this period will exhibit little but one monotonous round of 'wind so & so'. I can imagine nothing duller than people during a sea voyage—the same unvarying round of employment occupies them every day, and there is nothing to relieve the mind, or excite the fancy by its novelty.

I have heard and now partly seen how much a Ships Company resembles a State. There exists the same grades—the same heartburning after distinction, the same oppression of the poor and hatred of the rich, the same jealousy of the Aristocrats among

---

* *A Treatise On Sheep, with the best means for their improvement, general management, and the treatment of their diseases*, by the Scottish-born farmer and politician Ambrose Blacklock, had been first published earlier in 1838.

† *Marmion* and *The Lady of the Lake* were two of Sir Walter Scott's most popular long poems. They were written in the first decade of the nineteenth century.

‡ A famous line from Coleridge's *Rime of the Ancient Mariner* (1798).

themselves. And no where are all these more apparent or the cause of more annoyance than during a Sea Voyage of considerable length.

There are 2 sails in view, with every inch of canvas to the wind. They are very fine brigs*, seemingly going up to the Mediterranean.

9 December 1838. Sunday

Wind fair and a slight breeze. Our course is still south west but, as we shall soon have passed Ushant†, our course will be south. We then enter the Bay of Biscay, which I understand is a very stormy part of the Sea.

We had prayers on board this morning—but how different is it from the quiet scenes of Scotland on a Sabbath morning. With what feelings do I call to mind the duties that used to employ me on this morning—the dear Sabbath School, the Boys all kindness and docility, and the Pastor surveying his flock with feelings of pride, and at the same time of anxiety for their welfare. All these have made an impression on my mind never to be defaced or forgotten.

---

* A brig is a two-masted square-rigged ship.
† This is the English version of Ouessant, an island off Brittany that marks the north-westernmost point of mainland France.

I felt very thankful this morning to the God of all Grace for his goodness to me in time past & for having continued me in circumstances of outward comfort, and I prayed for a continuance of his favour—to me and to those whom I have ever upon my mind. I thought of C., who may be watching the sickbed of her Child—may God bless her and comfort her. How happy would I be if I could see her. I trust I shall.

I cannot imagine how she should be impressed in my favour. When I saw her, what was I? Young—my manners unpolished—my speech rude—altogether certainly a very unlikely person to make an impression in her mind. And the slanders she has heard of me, however false—all these circumstances combined would have made me most despicable in the eyes of any one not accustomed to looking beyond appearances and to judging for herself.

I swear I shall never deceive her. On the contrary I swear to God that I shall act by her as I ought when I consider the treatment I have had at her hands.

8 oClock. Breeze still moderate & fair. We are in Lat: 49° 15' N, Lon: 7° 44' W.

10 December 1838. Monday

Wind fair but very calm. We make little progress. Altho' the Sea is very pleasant, yet to a person longing for land it seems very tedious to be so idle. Vice appears in every form with us. I do indeed wonder how human beings can be so unmindful of the end for which they were made. Nothing else of consequence going on to day.

11 December 1838. Tuesday

Wind the same but still calmer to day. Consequently we almost lie like logs on the water. That is, our Ship lies—our course still south west.

I amuse myself with *anything*—which means *nothing*. Played my *maiden* game at chess with Mrs Elphick—she and her husband* are my fellow passengers, viz: in the Intermediate Cabin—and like myself have been much deceived as to its comforts. I feel for her every time I remember the fate of Mrs J. Hetherington—they are newly married. I was introduced to Mr Elphick in London and we were desired to cultivate terms of friendship.

Speaking of the Intermediate Cabin, I was recommended to take it to save money. I had expected much more comfort and I felt much disappointed at our want of accommodation, such as I had been accustomed to. But, having done as much as I could in the way of fitting up my Cabin, and having engaged a person to cook & wait on me, and as we get plenty

---

* William Elphick, chemist, and his wife, Susanna.

to eat & drink, and considering my determination to make money, I cannot think but I am right in *roughing* it, as it will prepare me for rough living if such is my lot. I am very well in health at present, indeed I have been seldom better.

In case this should fall into the hands of any person who may be situated as I am, I shall just say a few things for his direction.

1st Clothing. Cannot take too much—but at the least provide every thing necessary for a 4 months voyage, as there is no washing on board. Strong clothing is best.

2d Food. Take pickles preserves &c &c, to give a zest to the more substantial articles of food which are provided by the Ship—in fact too much cannot be taken of such things as may be more palatable than Ships stores.

3d Berth. Provide plenty of clothes to keep yourself clean—changes of Shirts &c. Fit up in such a way as you think will be most comfortable—washstand, shelves, table on which you can take your victuals &c. Cover your floor with a carpet or mat, and in short depend upon nothing being done for you. Do every thing for yourself & then you will not be disappointed.

But my opinion is that no married couple accustomed to genteel society can be comfortable but in the First Cabin. Young men may rough it but it is rough work, altho' it may be to their advantage afterwards. It is my first, and it shall be my last Sea Voyage in any part of the Ship but the 1st Cabin.

I wonder how Mrs Hetherington with her Brother and James Bryden came on during their voyage—they must have been deceived like me. They left Scotland in Augt to join their Brothers.

12 December 1838. Wednesday

Wind still fair—sky cloudy.

13 December 1838. Thursday

Lat 45°. A stiff breeze, but fair. We have this morning for the first time a good run—from 6 to 7 knots an hour. The Ship does not appear to sail fast but having fair winds we make considerable progress. People are still all healthy and now that more comfortable arrangements are made I feel more reconciled to a sea voyage than I thought I would become—and I realize the truth of the saying that no condition of life is really miserable. I feel already a slight difference of climate.

A Voyage to Australia

14 December 1838. Friday

Wind still fair but calm. Shoals of porpoises surround the Ship. Fired at them but without effect—they seem to rise to the surface being disturbed by the motion of the Vessel. I remarked[*] last night the beautiful luminous appearance of the sea. It is *very* beautiful.

I cannot express my surprise at the conduct of the passengers in the Steerage and also some profligates in another part of the Ship. I have had cause to mention this before. The commissioners are certainly very culpable in selecting such people and giving them a free passage. Why do they not send people convicted at once, instead of sending people who are no better than Convicts, and boast that none but free labourers of *good character* are sent to S. Australia. I shall not fail to let G.F.A. Co.[†] know how the interest they have taken in the prosperity of this Colony is followed up by the Commissioners. As for our *Cabin gentry* such conduct as theirs will bring along with it its own punishment—they give me no good opinion of human nature.

---

[*] That is, noted.

[†] Almost certainly a reference to George Fife Angas, initially a Colonization Commissioner, who resigned to float the South Australian Company as a major investor in, and financial support for, the establishment of the colony of South Australia.

Looked thro' my papers and letters—read & walked at intervals.

15 December 1838. Saturday

We are in Lat: 41° 20'. Wind calm but favourable. Vessel sails 2½ & 3 miles an hour—the Sun shone to day with much brightness, and altogether this has been the most pleasant day as regards weather that we have had.

About 4 p.m. the sky presented a singularly beautiful appearance—the Sun descending in the west unclouded, while light clouds floated along the sky in every other direction, thro' which the bright blue vault of heaven was to be seen contrasted with the ocean below, gilded by the setting sun. Led the mind to contemplate with admiration the beauties of nature and to look from nature up to natures God.

In the midst of this serenity a cloud appeared which soon obscured the scene. The ocean became troubled, and our Sailors trimmed their sails. The Rainbow appeared and, after a slight squall and a few drops of rain, the Scene was calm as before.

Tomorrow commences a new week—the 4th of my Voyage. May God enable me to spend his holy day aright, and continue his favour and protection in time to come. Every hour forces upon my mind recollections of the past and anticipations as to the future—and upon every consideration of the matter, I feel my resolutions of piety as regards morals and industry & perseverance as regards worldly affairs strengthened and confirmed. I already feel my heart bounding with a desire and hope of returning to Britain and, considering my youth, I think I may indulge the hope—but a very few years indeed will make many alterations among those I now remember with fond delight.

> *Wha kens, thought I, if friends I left,*
> *May still continue mine?*
> *Or, if I e'er again shall see*
> *The joys I left langsyne?**

16 December 1838. Sunday

Wind still fair and a good breeze. Lat: 39° 29'—which must be nearly opposite the straits of Gibraltor, but as we are in Lon: 16° we must be 400 miles from it. This day is most delightful—as warm and the Suns heat as great as on an April day in Scotland.

Our Capt read prayers in the morning. Only a few of the Passengers & none of the Sailors attended— why should they not all have been made to attend?

---

* This is from a popular Scottish song called 'Langsyne', credited to 'Miss Blamire'.

They spend the remainder of the day in amusing themselves, each according to his own mind. On my remonstrating with the Capt last Sunday evening—for amusing himself with a song—he told me the Sailors sabbath ended at 12 oClock. It is so according to his *log*—but certainly not according to his bible.

A laughable farce occurred last night. One of the young Gents had been displaying a very beautiful well curled head of hair which had given him an air of great gentility ever since he came on board. But unluckily the sport ran upon endeavouring to detect and pluck grey hairs—the consequence & glory of age, of which however none of them can boast as they seem to be one and all unacquainted with 30 years. And upon my gentlemans head being, much against his will, submitted to the scrutiny, at one pull the whole hair was separated from his *pow** in shape of a wig—and left his head despoiled of all its *glory*. The poor fellow cannot resume his wig and has suffered no little grief from the discovery, while his personal appearance is much altered—he has afforded no little amusement. Were I disposed to moralise I have here a subject—but I content myself with stating it, and leave every person to deduce a moral for himself.

There is among the Steerage Passengers a man

---

* British slang for a head.

named McLean* from Argyleshire with his wife and
3 children. I had marked him as a decent man (of
whom we have but few on board) and are become
acquainted—I have been of some little service to him,
in the way of giving him from my own allowance
(which is more than I choose to use) a little wine
for his wife when sick, lending him books to read
&c. Surprised was I to find that he was a Servant
of the Stewarts of Fasnacloich Appin†, the near relations & Clansmen of my own friend and patron C.
Stewart—this circumstance is sufficient to call forth
an interest for him in my services such as I can render
him. He has been induced to leave his native hills
and go out as Shepherd to a Mr Duncan who has
sailed a month ago—he seems to know his business
& I think will do well.

The consequence of certain of our Gents choosing
to be found about the Decks at rather late hours
in company with certain of our female Emigrants
begin already to prove not much to their liking.
I think we shall have some precious 'kick ups' before
long—their conduct has been so glaring that I cld
not refrain from noticing it here, perhaps more than
I ought. Good conduct must & certainly does bring

---

* Alexander McLean of Achnacree, Argyllshire.
† Appin is a remote coastal district of the Scottish West
Highlands. It is the traditional home of one of the major
branches of the Clan Stewart.

its own reward, both in the estimation of our fellow men and in the peace of conscience it affords to the Individual—even supposing it were not required by the laws of the God that made us.

17 December 1838. Monday

Wind fair and a good breeze. We make from 5 to 7 miles an hour. Passed the Azores Islands* but we have steered so far west that we are completely out of the sight of land—and have missed seeing the whole coast of the countries we have passed and have only seen one sail this fortnight. Indeed I can't tell what has become of every wonder that is to be seen and is usually seen in sailing along our track. I have not seen a bird all last week, nor a fish excepting a few porpoises. Indeed I am inclined to think that we have been hitherto more than usually dull. We are however steering so as to be within sight of Madeira† and I hope will be a little relieved from our monotony.

---

* The Azores are nine volcanic Portuguese islands situated in the middle of the North Atlantic Ocean, located about 1500 kilometres west of Lisbon and about 4000 kilometres east of the New Jersey coast. In truth, the *Planter* sailed so far to the *east* of the Azores that they could not be sighted.

† Another group of Portuguese volcanic islands, 870 kilometres south-west of Lisbon, about 580 kilometres directly west of Morocco. Latitude: 33° N; longitude: 17° W.

18 December 1838. Tuesday

A good breeze to day—we make from 6 to 8½ knots.
The Vessel rolls to day a good deal owing to the swell
from the east—tomorrow we expect to get a sight of
Madeira. We are now near the latitude of the country
of my adoption, S. Australia.* It is very mild indeed,
rather too close at night except upon deck.

About 11 oClock a shower of rain fell as mild as
an April shower in Scotland.

19 December 1838. Wednesday

Calm. We make very little progress. Spent the day
in reading & any other way to put off the time. The
evening very beautiful & spent by many of us *'not in
prayer'*. There were two sails in sight this morning.

20 December 1838. Thursday

Dead calm—the Sea is as smooth as oil, and with
the morning Sun reflected from its bosom presents
a spectacle on which I could gaze for hours. There
are innumerable sorts of fishes sporting round the
Ship. Our Capt saw or imagined he saw a turtle asleep
on the surface and with much haste lowered a boat

---

* Well, latitude 33° *south* runs through South Australia.

to secure him—he managed to get the boat down in about an hour afterwards, when I suppose the turtle (if such there was) was some half dozen miles astern.

This morning we descried a speck on the horizon which turned out a Sail. It has gained on us all day and is now distinctly seen to be an English Ship steering our course. She has kept to windward and will be past us before midnight and probably out of sight in the morning. Indeed I think there never was a slower sailing Vessel than the 'Planter'. It is impossible on the whole to imagine in my opinion a Vessel worse adapted to the Voyage than ours and, if we take into account the Capt and Passengers too, I am sure we are a pretty mess.

The Capt is a young man—married*, '*but as a Sailor*' —and a person shewing more silliness & weakmindedness I never saw. The Passengers I have already mentioned and altogether we are a *precious Set*. I wish we were safely landed, which in all appearance will not be in any usual length of time. Of course there are exceptions among us—but I do think that they are fewer than can generally be found among 120 persons—and while the Capt encourages vice as he does it may easily be imagined how the matter goes.

---

* The marriage of Thomas Beazley and Temperance Arrowsmith is recorded as having taken place on 10 July 1835 at St John's Church Hackney, London.

We seem to be as far off Madeira to day as ever, and according to their observations to day we must be 100 miles west of it, altho the Capt said yesterday that he intended to go so near as to admit of the people coming off to sell their fruit, which it seems they are always ready to do.

21 December 1838. Friday

This morning is as calm as yesterday. The helm is deserted and we are completely idle. If we don't get a breeze, we may lie here nobody knows how long. There is enough of dullness and monotony; indeed we are quite the reverse of happy and cannot tell the reason why we are unhappy. The Ship seen yesterday was barely visible as a speck on the horizon this morning. She had passed us in the night. I would indeed like well to be able to enter into the feelings of Byron when he penned these beautiful lines—

> *Oh, who can tell, save he whose heart hath tried,*
> *And danced in triumph o'er the waters wide,*
> *The exulting sense—the pulse's maddening play,*
> *That thrills the wanderer of that trackless way?**

---

* From the First Canto of Lord Byron's epic poem *The Corsair* (1814).

I heard accounts this morning of several cases of sickness on board. None of them considered serious.

22 December 1838. Saturday

The morning calm. We had steered all night so as to get in sight of Madeira to adjust the Ship's chronometers—and about 9 oClock we discerned between two parting clouds the outline of the land dim in the distance. A breeze sprang up and we approached gradually and with feelings of no ordinary description from the appearance of land emerging from the ocean, and situated above the waves—while the Sea beat against it on every side. The coast on the north is very high, I would say 300 feet perpendicular, and immediately above the precipice the land rises by a rapid ascent, and ends in a high ridge overtopping a blue cloud which hovered on the middle of the ridge.

As we approach nearer, the white houses become visible & in the centre a Convent which speaks the religion of the Island. At last we can discern the green vineyards among the hills, and at every mile along the coast a ravine made by the water running down from the high land ends in a waterfall into the blue profound beneath. It is impossible to describe the beauty of the scene, as it assumes various appearances according to the distance. It is famous for its wine

& belongs to Portugal. Poor Mr Beattie of Crieve[*] died here whither he had gone for the recovery of his health.

We pass it on the west at a distance of about 8 miles—and as it is just about sun setting, no boats will come off so we shall not get any fruit. The coast is lower on the west, but the approach of evening prevents us seeing it.

8 oClock. The breeze has left us and we are literally becalmed off Madeira. If we have no breeze we may still be within reach in the morning. I shall quote 'Thomson' here and then proceed to note a circumstance which, tho' disgraceful beyond measure, is a relief from the tedium of a Sea Voyage.

The fruitful fields laugh with abundant produce,
And the four seasons woven into one,
And that one season a perpetual spring,
Gives life and cheerfulness to all around
The noxious reptile finds no footing here;
But birds of song and plumage various

---

[*] In 1831 the parliament of Westminster had passed an act to empower the judges of the Courts of Sessions in Scotland to take account of the debts of the Estate of Crieve in the counties of Dumfries and Roxburgh. Part of the problem appears to have been a 'Deed of Entail made by Thomas Beattie of Crieve Esquire, now deceased'. Probably this is the gentleman to whom Bell refers here.

Carol the live-long day, and here, in search
Of health, the emaciated, care-worn
European seeks repose, and wards the sting of death.[*]

Now for my story. Well, we have on board two Messrs Nicholson†, Cabin Passengers. They have got two dogs, and this evening as usual they had loosed them to give them an airing. The dogs, like other dogs, differed & began to fight. Their Masters, tho' brothers, in consequence lost their humour and each assumed the side of his own dog. Of course there was little fair play going, and the brothers thought of enforcing it by blows. Hence a dog fight & a gentleman brother fight, both at once—what a variety. I was afraid I had formed too bad an opinion of our people, but I think this will bear me out. Of course it ended—and I was shocked to hear the one utter vows of vengeance against his brother, who appeared to take a more proper view of the matter.

The Capt endeavoured to keep the peace of the Ship but with a feeble arm. We are in a pretty mess

---

* I have been unable to discover these lines among James Thomson's extensive writings. However, by some kind of odd coincidence, in 1840 James Marshall published in London a book called *Twenty Years Experience in Australia: Being the evidence of disinterested and respectable residents*. It is a compilation of the experiences of many people, but it quotes these exact lines from Thomson in its description of Madeira.

† Arthur and Robert Nicholson.

tonight from this shameful circumstance—I can't tell to what it will lead next. I had thought the Nicholsons among our most respectable people—they are natives of Edinburgh. The one has a wife and one child on board.

23 December 1838. Sunday

Fine breeze this morning & has been since 12 oClock last night. Madeira scarce visible—and almost as far distant as when first discovered yesterday morning. I would have liked exceedingly to have seen more of it but it is now passed and perhaps I may never be so near it again. The Sun shines very warm to day and Divine service is performed under an awning.

I am wont to carry my thoughts backwards to past occurrences more upon this morning than any other and I fell into a fit of musing, and almost before I was aware of it found myself shedding a flood of tears. With all my fortitude I could not restrain them, and again & again would the memory of some one of my relations or friends separated from me, perhaps for ever, force itself upon me and cause my tears to flow afresh, until I had recourse to the source of all consolation & poured out my heart in prayer to God for a blessing upon them all. I felt ashamed of my weakness but still I cannot restrain my emotion upon every recollection of those who are near and dear to me.

Breeze increased in the afternoon and we are getting on beautifully. How much I long for the great Sabbaths I used to spend in Scotland.

24 December 1838. Monday

Beautiful breeze from the north east. We make 8 miles an hour. A Ship seen to the windward of us. Weather rather cloudy but at intervals the Sun shines very bright. Yesterday commenced the fifth week of our voyage and thank God it has been a favourable one hitherto.

I am surprised to find so many people all going out to farm, and altogether ignorant of it. Of 6 people going out as Cabin Passengers there is not one knows anything whatever of the matter—and still all intend to farm.* They are people who do not appear as if they would do much good any where, at least all but one or two. And the Servants they have with them, sent out by the Commissioners, are as ignorant as themselves—people whom they have got to accompany them by promises they will never fulfil.

---

* The 1840 statistical return for South Australia names four *Planter* cabin passengers as having established farms around Adelaide: the Nicholson brothers, Captain John Holmes, and Joseph Nias.

25 December 1838. Tuesday— Christmas day

We have a continuation of the breeze—and are now making 200 Miles in 24 hours. Weather cloudy and not very hot.

Our passengers make every effort that is in their power to get plum pudding and roast Beef—but such a mess. Pudding of coarse flour, Suet & Raisins, boiled in salt water, is not indeed very palatable. They all however appear clean and in good spirits, which pleases me most. The Capt treated them all to a glass of rum and water.

I have enjoyed myself a good deal, but more from seeing what was going forward than any share I took in it. I had never been accustomed to know much difference between this and any other day—and tho' fully alive to the important event commemorated, yet I enjoy much more the pleasure I feel from seeing the 'Planter' bound over the waves, and the cheering hope of reaching Adelaide and a speedy passage, than in eating and drinking.

I have spent a very pleasant hour in the evening with Mr & Mrs Elphick. They are worthy people and I feel very happy in their society. Our Cabin Gents have had a good dinner & plenty of wine, and have got upon deck to quarrel as usual. I understand that they ushered in Christmas eve in rather a *'rum'* manner last night.

About 12 oClock we descried a Vessel to leeward about 20 Miles distant. We gradually neared each other till within 6 or 8 miles when she shewed her colours and they were English, but we could not make out her number. It is believed however that she is the 'Buckinghamshire' which was to sail from London to South Australia with Passengers on 10 December. She has passed us like all the rest and will land her Passengers some fortnight before us.[*] She is already out of sight.

I cannot pass my notes of the day without a remembrance of how happy my friends in Britain will be—and still I am afraid they are unhappy. At Peelhouses[†] there is no attention paid to Christmas— at Workington their family circle is sadly contracted and perhaps may be more so before this time, tho' I wish it may be otherwise. And I shall conclude with wishing them all many happy returns of this season.

---

[*] The *Buckinghamshire* arrived in Adelaide on 22 March 1839.
[†] Peelhouses Farm is an ancient holding north of the town of Lockerbie. It is possible that this is the establishment to which James Bell refers. It is close to Dryfesdale, where James Bell's family seems to have lived.

While I am writing I hear a noise and run on deck to see what is the matter. It is only a 'regular' Stand up fight between two of our Cabin Passengers. I shall say no more about it.

26 December 1838. Wednesday

We are in Lat: 25° 25' N, Lon: 21° 15' W. Breeze still fresh and favourable. I have a slight headache caused by being awakened by a dreadful *row* among the Cabin gents upon deck at 3 oClock this morning. They were all tipsy & quarrelling, singing, dancing, making love, all at once—and the Capt worst.

I admire innocent and rational amusement as much as any person. But I never saw people indulge in every criminal pleasure & sinful crime so unblushingly as the Passengers on board this vessel. I have been obliged to check the advances of several of them & avoid a friendship which in ordinary circumstances might be of use, but which would certainly be a disgrace. I do not speak rashly or unwarrantably when I say so.

A flying fish lighted on deck this morning. A number of porpoises sporting round the bows. They tried to harpoon some but could not.

8 p.m. Breeze delightful. The last night's *wassailers* just making their exit from their Cabins for the first time to day, and already I am annoyed by their

loud laugh and coarse jests. I am always of opinion however that it is best to meet them in the most affable manner.

27 December 1838. Thursday

Still a fine breeze—and we expect a continuance of it till we get across the line.

This morning there appeared a sail evidently bearing down upon us from windward. The Capt was very suspicious of her character. She however upon nearing us altered her course and we have got her out of sight. Our belief however is that she was a Slaver—inhuman traffic. It appeared to us that she had 'windsails' to convey the air below, perhaps to a number of poor wretches torn from their native land. We have nothing but small arms on board and would fall an easy prey to any enemy. She cost us many an anxious look—as we are just about the place for pirates. If we are so fortunate as to have this trade wind as strong as it is at present we shall get on fast.

No sickness on board except a child, of water in its head.* I understand it will soon terminate its existence.

---

* Hydrocephalus is more usually called 'water on the brain'; an accumulation of cerebrospinal fluid causes the head to swell.

Merrily, merrily, goes the bark,
Before the gale she bounds;
So darts the dolphin from the shark
Or the deer before the hounds.[*]

28 December 1838. Friday

Breeze still all we can wish. Child died this morning of Hydrocephalos, or water in the head; this disorder is very seldom cured, and there was no chance of its being so by our Doctor. It was buried at 4 oClock p.m. The passengers seemed a good deal impressed by the scene, & I trust a good many of them took into consideration their own latter end.

It has been very hot to day. We are in Lat about 20° north. The Parents of the child are in much affliction—they are labouring people, and thus been made to see 'Love's labour lost'. I have had the good fortune to have a very good airy Cabin and feel the comforts of it now. No sails in sight to day.

29 December 1838. Saturday

Still going on well. The sky is most beautiful by day and quite delightful at night. The moon shines with

---

[*] From the Fourth Canto of Sir Walter Scott's *The Lord of the Isles* (1815).

extreme lustre *in the north*, the planets much larger in appearance than I have been accustomed to see them, while the whole are reflected from the Sea, presenting to the eye a picture on which it loves to repose with rapture & almost unceasingly, and leads the mind to contemplation while it sets all the passions at rest and spreads a feeling of pleasure & happiness over the whole soul. These scenes please me beyond measure and are not a little enhanced by the expression of the feelings of Mr & Mrs Elphick who are able to enter with me into all my admiration of the sublime.

The Capt has handcuffed a person to day and set him to live on bread & water. He is one of the Steerage passengers and his crime is refusing to do what he had no business to do, but what he ought to have done out of regard to the comfort of himself and fellow passengers. The Capt made far too much talk and foolish parade about it. The fellow remains obstinate and persuasion would do more with him than force.

We hope to see the Cape Verd* Islands in a day or two. I have been reading Goldsmith & Gray† to

---

* This was the spelling at the time of what today are the Cape Verde Islands, which are mid-Atlantic and about 570 kilometres from West Africa. When they were colonised by the Portuguese in the fifteenth century they were uninhabited volcanic outcrops, but they later became important to slave traders.

† Thomas Gray is today best remembered for his *Elegy Written in a Country Churchyard* (1751). The multi-talented Oliver

day—discover new charms in *The Deserted Village* of the former.

30 December 1838. Sunday

Wind stronger to day—and our course being more direct south gives us it more upon our beam, which renders the motion very unpleasant. I feel very unwell to day.

31 December 1838. Monday

Rather more pleasant to day. My sickness is very unpleasant—towards the afternoon I feel much better, it proceeded from my head and stomach. This is the last day of another year and is a season that particularly calls for reflection & self examination. I trust I shall spend my next more happily. I wish it was over as I would not be surprised to see the whole Ships Company tipsy.

Another year! another year,
Is borne by time away;
Nor pauses yet his swift career,

Goldsmith is remembered for his poetry—including his pastoral poem, *The Deserted Village* (1770)—his novel, *The Vicar of Wakefield* (1766), his play, *She Stoops to Conquer* (1773), and his essays.

Nor tires his wing, nor makes he here
*E'en one short hours delay.**

But—

But hurries on, and round, and round,
The wheel of life is sped;
Unnoted oft, until rebound
Upon the ear, the startling sound
Another year has fled!

Whoever said, 'tis New Year's day
With unmixed care or glee?
For hope still paints the future gay,
And memory o'er the past will stray,
With sorrowing constancy.

E. Dickinson

1 January 1839. Tuesday

As I anticipated we have had a sad time of it. To explain it I shall just mention what passed during last night.

At 8 p.m. plenty of *rum punch*. To prevent giving offence I was obliged to join the party in the 2d

---

* From *The Mamluk* (1830) by the English poet, Eleanor Dickinson (not to be confused with America's own Emily Dickinson, who was in fact born in 1830).

Cabin—the glasses or rather *mugs* were deep, and the noise astounding. The *Punch* soon began to operate and the whole of the Ships Officers were *all but under the table*, except the Capt who was satisfied with drinking the health of our part of the Ship in wine and water. When 8 bells (12 oClock) struck, I & Mr Elphick had managed (by quietly passing our glasses to Mrs E., who disposed of their contents into the slop basin and returned them) to be able to call ourselves sober.

8 bells however was the signal for a general salute, and every one who could boast a rusty musket had her loaded and appeared on deck. The bell again tolled and off went the rusty muskets amidst roars of applause.

So much for the welcome given to the New Year. The order 'below' was then given but was complied with by few. I retired however to 'try to sleep'; but after about an hour submitting to all but being suffocated by the heat & fumes of the place, I determined to find more air and wrapping my cloak about me got upon deck.

There I found it every where covered with people tipsy—and round the hatchway the doctor with some ½ doz more gents lying (they cd not stand) singing or rather roaring all manner of songs and in regular

'Haymarket style'* making *night hideous.* I found however a place in the long boat, where I laid down but was still unable to sleep on account of the noise. Towards morning the breeze freshened and I thought of again trying my bed. I found the hatchway as before surrounded by the wassailers more noisy than before. I went to bed and in half an hour was asleep.

I rose this morning at 5 and bathed—but with a sad headache. The man at the wheel is unable to steer and the mate has taken it from him and put him in irons. Two more sailors appear at the bows to try themselves at fighting and altogether it has been such a scene as I never witnessed. At 12 noon the passengers are not all appeared and soda water is in great demand.

I shall dismiss this disagreeable part of my remarks by giving it as my opinion that there was never so much debauchery among the same number of people as has taken place among us these 24 hours past and the discipline of the Capt & Surgeon Superintendant have been worse than none, as *they* have set an example to all the rest. One of the passengers the other day asked the doctor if all Emigrant Ships were like this. The Doctor stared.

---

* Presumably a style of singing associated with the famous Haymarket Theatre in London.

The past and the future again occupy my thoughts. With the former I associate friends—and in the latter much that is dark and unlovely, tho' not unenlivened by hope. The present only is mine—in it I am *not unhappy* and not ungrateful. So I hope my friends are all the same and I wish them all many, many happy New Years—and not less than any of them do I extend my good wishes to her for whom I feel sentiments of much respect.

2 January 1839. Wednesday

Had a good nights sleep and feel very well to day. The wind is still the same and we have been going on splendidly altho' 2 or 3 miles an hour less than many ships would have done. About noon saw a flock of birds skimming along the Sea—this talks of land, but we ought to be 1000 miles from it else we are sadly out in our calculation. Our Lat is 8½° N so we shall cross the Line this week. Thermometer is 80 in the shade. It is very hot below—but pretty airy on deck and not uncomfortable.

3 January 1839. Thursday

Breeze now considerably less and the heat increases much—thermometer 85—and we are afraid of being becalmed upon the Line. I slept on Deck last night.

It was quite warm enough without any covering. In the evening I was much gratified by the beautiful appearance of the fishes as they came to the surface—a gleam of lights which, extending on all sides for miles, gave the Sea the appearance of being illuminated. I suppose a number of them were dolphins. Lat 5½°.

4 January 1839. Friday

A calm. The Sea as smooth as oil. Every person on board bathed this morning. A breeze sprang up about 10 oClock and we are now making about 2 or 3 miles an hour. It is very hot.

I cannot describe all that strikes the mind of a young Voyager on first entering a tropical climate. The disagreeables of my situation disappear before the interesting scenes in which I have been & expect to be. We did not pass the Cape Verd Islands near enough to see them.

5 January 1839. Saturday

Breeze very light in the morning. It increased during the day, but sunk into a calm in the evening and left us literally in the midst of a furnace of sulphur. Thunder rolled in the distance and the constant flashes of the electric fluid amidst the darkness, which from the absence of moon was very dense, was awfully grand and majestic. It lighted up the quarter of the heavens from whence it proceeded and, as it merged in the Ocean like a solid body of flame, left the beholder lost in wondering amazement, and told of the power of him in whose hands is the bolt of heaven.

It rained a little during the evening which was indeed very refreshing.

6 January 1839. Sunday

Last night again we had beautiful lightning, but not so much as the evening before. The appearance was not so grand. We had a slight breeze in the morning. But it is now 1 oClock p.m.—calm and the sails hang useless about the masts. Saw a number of fishes called black fish—large unsightly animals, they rolled about in the water quite near the Ship and had a few rifle balls directed at them, to the serious disturbance of 'their day of rest'.

Had a form of divine service at 11 oClock a.m. but, from the way in which it was gone about, it was well calculated to inspire those who seemed to join in with any feelings but those of devotion. Cowper's satire falls far short of what they merit who conduct the Service of God on board the 'Planter'.

Behold the picture! Is it like?—Like whom?
The things that mount the rostrum with a skip,
And then skip down again; pronounce a text;
Cry—hem; and reading what they never wrote,
Just fifteen minutes, huddle up their work
And with a well-bred whisper close the scene!*

And what can we say of those who, as soon as the 'irksome' task is done, return to sports more childish than would engage a boy of 12 summers while they combine the vice and heartless depravity so charac-teristic of those just escaped from Billingsgate†, while by their example they loose the bonds of common decency among those over whom they ought to have control, and Vice flows unchecked through all its channels. Nor is this exaggerated but on the contrary, were I to mention all that I could prove, it would seem incredible to any one but such as have, like me, been so often disgusted with the proceedings of the Capt and others on board the 'Planter'.

---

* The English poet, William Cowper, in 1785 wrote *The Task: A Poem, in Six Books*—6000 lines of blank verse as a discursive meditation on the blessings of nature, the retired life and religious faith, with attacks on slavery, blood sports, fashion-able frivolity and lukewarm clergy. The quoted passage is from Book 1: *The Sofa.*

† In the nineteenth century, Billingsgate was notorious for its fish market. The raucous cries of its vendors gave rise to 'billingsgate' as a synonym for profanity or offensive language.

We are in Lat 3½° N. It is very hot indeed and, while almost burnt up by the heat of the Sun, there is such a dullness and listlessness oppress the whole faculties of both mind and body that one feels incapable of the least exertion. I am still in the enjoyment of tolerable health.

7 January 1839. Monday

It has rained all last night with thunder and lightning at intervals. A number of passengers had lain down to sleep on deck and had a fresh water bath for a change, while mattresses and bedding got completely drenched. The rain fell in torrents but not more so than I have seen it in Scotland. The Sailors saved a considerable quantity of rain water which we all preferred to our other stock, which is now getting not very good.

About 11 oClock the rain abated and a slight breeze sprang up which continued all day while the sky, becoming unclouded, gave us the heat of the Sun unmitigated by any friendly medium. We have made about a degree since yesterday.

8 January 1839. Tuesday

Calm and without a cloud in the morning. Towards midday a breeze. We are in Lat 1½° and now very nearly approach the Line.

It has just hitherto been as was expected, viz a trade wind from Madeira to about 3 deg. from the Line. Then calm and light winds for 3 deg. on each side, after which we expect another trade wind to carry us straight round the Cape.

A Ship homeward bound passed us at 6 this morning. It is believed that she belongs to France. She was an acceptable sight, being the only one for a good many days. We exchanged signals, but she was not within speaking.

There are no more cases of sickness on board except 2 delicate females (one the wife of Mr Nicholson the *dogfighter*) who have become very weak from Sea sickness. It is very warm now, at times almost intolerable. Oh for a little of the frost and snow I am sure is now in Scotland, to brace the nerves once more.

9 January 1839. Wednesday

Calm. Last evening about 5 oClock we observed ahead a Vessel homeward bound, and our Capt immediately made up his mind to speak her. We had just half an hour as she was coming down with full sail, and a good breeze, while we were sailing about 5 miles an hour. But no tongue can express the anxiety and bustle that ensued.

Writing desks, pens & paper were soon put in requisition, and before 15 minutes had elapsed there appeared many an anxious face with a letter grasped in a hand quivering with emotion, which was increased as the beautiful little Brig swept along side. When in answer to our enquiries we found that she was bound to Jersey, and promised to carry our letters, she immediately hove too, and we took in all sail and dispatched a boat with many a hurried note the harbinger of good tidings to anxious friends and relatives.

When our boat returned we found that she was a Brig of 120 tons from Rio Janeira* to Jersey—her name 'Medusa'. They got a few cigars from her and repaid her by adjusting her Longitude, she having no chronometer† on board and being 2 deg. wrong.

I wrote two hurried scrawls, one to C.P. and the other to Brother Chas. which I hope they will receive in safety. I never felt such a sensation of pleasure and so much excitement as I experienced in the occasion.

---

*   Captain James Cook called it 'Rio de Janeira'.

†   To understand the importance of having an accurate marine chronometer on board see Dava Sobel's acclaimed book, *Longitude*.

We are just upon the Line to day and the Sailors are preparing to initiate the *new comers* into the dominion of Neptune. I have made my peace with the Deity who, in common with all sea Gods, is rather fond of *strong waters*—but I suppose we shall have some precious foolery before the day is out. I shall say a few words as to it tomorrow when I see the furthest of it. It is very hot to day.

10 January 1839. Thursday

Yesterday about 10 oClock a.m. the ceremony of shaving commenced.* Neptune had come on board the night before, and this morning appeared accompanied by his Lady, and followed by a tremendous bear. Neptune had in his grasp a ponderous trident in the shape of a harpoon, and the bear was covered with a sheep skin. The deities were seated in a chair of State, mounted on a splendid car (or hatch) & drawn by a number of inferior deities who afterwards officiated

---

* The 'Crossing the Line' ceremony began as a ritual in the Royal Navy, supposedly as an ordeal for those who had never previously crossed the equator, so as to ensure they were capable of undergoing long sea journeys. It slowly transformed itself into an entertainment for passengers.

The ceremony was in the hands of Neptune (by tradition played by the oldest sailor on board) and his Queen, Amphitrite (a sailor in drag), plus others, including the barber and usually two bears as attendants.

as his Barber, Secretary &c &c. Their Majesties dismissed their car and received the 'Planter' which they were pleased to say they had long expected and, having tasted a glass of wine to the health and prosperity of all on board, proceeded to the side of a pond of water, found on the Lee side of the deck, and took their Seats.

The pond was formed by filling some spare sails & a tarpaulin and into it they put the Bear. All the passengers had been sent below, and on their names being read over the constables were sent in search of them one after another. Upon their being apprehended, they were blindfolded and brought before their Majesties who asked them a few questions such as what is your age? &c &c. They were seated and the Barber proceeded to lather them—the poor with tar, the rich with something else—and then shaved them quite close with a piece of iron hoop. Then by way of a wash they were plunged head and ears into the water where the bear was ready to give them a friendly hug or two, and then they were allowed to have the use of their eyes and make their escape while they were washed by a dozen friendly hands standing ready with buckets of water for the occasion.

I had bought my admission into Neptunes dominions by an easier way than shaving & ducking, but as all were trying it I took a fancy to it too and was shaved (not with tar) and ducked. But not so the poor steerage passengers—on their being sent below, they thought that nothing less than death was intended, and when his Majesties officers arrived they found them armed with offensive weapons and ready to fight for their lives while their wives were going one by one into hysterics till the fury should be over.

The officers (Sailors) would have proceeded with their duty but the Capt interfered, not without losing his temper and calling them a parcel of 'disagreeable brutes'—that he had done all he could to make them comfortable during the Voyage but 'by God' he would make 'their lives miserable during the rest of it'. The Sailors passed them; and restrained the Shaving to such as chose it and only McLean the Highlandman (by my persuasion) tried it.

When it was over every thing was dried up and the evening was spent in singing, dancing and something worse too. Two of the Sailors—or rather the Rum they drunk—were at striking each other and the Capts interference seemed to be of little consequence to restore order.

There is however peace again to day. It is quite calm and the Ship going round and round just as she chooses, while the Sun shines with great warmth. The heat is almost insufferable. We are in Lat: $0°\ 38'$ N, altho we crossed yesterday *according to Neptune*.

The Planets last night were seen shining with great lustre, and a patch of light I observed for several evenings past struck my mind as being some comet[*] whose reflection was the cause of it. I have been scrawling for a good many days past at arms length and on my knee. It is impossible to write below and there is no convenience on deck.

11 January 1839. Friday

A light breeze this morning, and our course is south west by south. It is exceedingly hot to day—115 deg. in the Sun. In Scotland I suppose it is about one third of that height—and I will say for my part that the one is more pleasant than the other.

The Capt has frequently made unsolicited proffers of service to me, and last night again told me that every thing in his Cabin was at my service. I have never yet drawn on his generosity; neither will I, as I know well that he wishes as little as may be said about this voyage as possible and his last night's proffer followed on a desire that I would say nothing about a complaint that had been made to me by McLean, that some of the Emigrants had been served with Grog, which they drank (no doubt following the example of their betters) and, thereby becoming tipsy, had given no little annoyance and afterwards *'mistaken their berths'* &c &c.

---

[*] It is possible that Bell saw Biela's Comet, which was visible faintly in 1839.

12 January 1839. Saturday

We have got again into a trade wind and have a good run. I suppose we are rather fortunate in having got so soon out of the calms and light winds upon the Line.

Tomorrow commences our 8th week and at the end of it we should have accomplished one half of our journey but we will be far short and, unless we have very good winds, it will yet be a long dreary voyage—and will try my patience, as I am already quite satisfied with the length of it. I will need a good deal of hope to enable me to endure it.

Hope flings her beam when the waves are foaming,
And the trembler hails the welcome ray;
Hope cheers the heart of the wanderer roaming
*O'er stranger lands, from his home away.**

13 January 1839. Sunday

We have still this morning a fine breeze. We are got into the south east trade wind, which blows till we reach 30° and then we shall be out of the tropics. Our present intention is to call at an Island in 37°

---

* The poem 'What is hope?' by 'T.W.A.' appeared in *Ward's Miscellany and Family Magazine*, 1837.

called Tristan Da' Cunha for provisions, fresh water
&c &c. But the winds or our Capts mind, which in
regard to stability are pretty nearly equal, may make
this otherwise.

Divine Service was gone thro' to day by about one
tenth of the crew and passengers. No more chose to
attend.

14 January 1839. Monday

The Trader is as usual true to her post this morning
and the 'Planter' is availing herself of her constancy,
in so far as a Ship built according to the construction
of a Dutchman (viz broad bottomed) can and is
bearing as motley a burden as ever floated on Salt
Water, at the rate of about 5 miles an hour. We are
in about 6° S Lat and 29° W Lon.

The heat is not intense. With the breeze and the
clouds that are constantly passing over the Sun, it is
much mitigated. 19 more deg. will set us once more
into a Temperate Zone. I trust we shall be allowed
to pass thro' the tropics without experiencing any
of the effects of a tropical hurricane as described
by Thomson.

> *But chief at Sea, whose every flexile wave*
> *Obeys the blast, the aerial tumult swells.*
> *In the dread ocean, undulating wide,*

Beneath the radiant line that girts the globe,
The circling Typhon*, whirl'd from point to point,
Exhausting all the rage of all the sky
And dire Ecnephia, reign. Amid the heavens,
Falsely serene, deep in a cloudy speck**
Compress'd, the mighty tempest brooding dwells:
Of no regard, save to the skilful eye,
Fiery and foul, the small prognostic hangs
Aloft, or on the promontory's brow
Muster its force. A faint deceitful calm,
A fluttering gale, the demon sends before,
To tempt the spreading sail. Then down at once
Precipitant, descends a mingling mass
Of roaring winds, and flame, and rushing floods.
In wild amazement fix'd, the sailor stands.
Art is too slow: by rapid fate oppress'd,
His broad-winged vessel drinks the whelming tide,
Hid in the bosom of the black abyss.†

* Typhon and Ecnephia, names of particular storms
  or hurricanes, known only between the tropics.
  [Footnote in original]

** The small speck is called by Sailors the Oxeye,
  being in appearance at first no bigger. [Footnote
  in original]

---

† From James Thomson's *The Seasons: Summer.*

15 January 1839. Tuesday

A continuance of the south east trade wind. It is very warm to day and the Sun fast becoming vertical. But with the glorious splendor of the evening, what can unfold?

The Sun set in unclouded beauty over the famed 'land of the West' and so soon as he had disappeared beneath the horizon a thousand blue clouds, like trees of the greatest loneliness, appeared to stud and diversify the Sea of gold formed by the reflection of the bright orb of day which, tho' lost to our vision, yet by this testified that he was still going on his course enlightening other worlds. The whole appearance presented to my mind the idea of a lake studded with Islands, on which the eye rested with delight, while the ever varying scene, becoming darker and more sombre as the shades of evening increased and tinctured the view with streaks of red or purple, called up innumerable flights of fancy, or left the mind absorbed in contemplation of and meditation upon the beauties of nature and led the thoughts upward to nature's God.

Here there is almost no twilight and so soon as the Sun is set the world is involved in darkness and with all its beauties a tropical climate is deprived of an hour to me the loveliest the day has to boast of.

16 January 1839. Wednesday

Wind still fair and a fair breeze. It is more easterly to day and our course more direct south. It was before to day south west. It is exceedingly hot and even under an awning is almost insufferable. Our Lat: is 9° 30' S, Lon: 32° W which on referring to the Map places us within 250 miles of St Lucia* in South America. We expect however that when out of the tropics we shall have a westerly wind to carry us more directly on our voyage.

People are still all well on board. I have just been thinking to day upon the remarkable places, rivers &c in South America and their Geography and history—and I cannot I think convey my meaning better nor perhaps employ my time to more advantage than by transcribing Thomson.†

No less thy world, Columbus, drinks, refresh'd,
The lavish moisture of the melting year.
Wide o'er his isles, the branching Oronoque
Rolls a brown deluge; and the native drives

---

* South America is studded with many places with the name St Lucia. Perhaps this was the city in Brazil of that name. It was certainly not the well-known West Indian island, which is north of the equator.

† Bell then dutifully, if slightly inaccurately, transcribed more than five dozen lines from Thomson's *The Seasons: Summer* (1727), beginning with the words reproduced here.

To dwell aloft on life-suff'ring trees,
At once his home, his robe, his food, his arms.
Swell'd by a thousand streams, impetuous hurl'd
From all the roaring Andes, huge descends
The mighty Orellana . . .

17 January 1839. Thursday

We are still careering it before the Trader—and are looking forward to getting beyond 'Capricorn' and then to Tristan D'Cunha, where we hope to have an opportunity of stretching our legs for an hour or two while the Ship is taking in her stock of fresh provisions.

There has been a complete turn over among our Cabin Gents, originating in nothing of more importance than a jealousy of one another in regard to the 'not much to be envied' affections of some 'frail fair ones' sent by the Commissioners for the accommodation of the public, at least I can see little else they are use for. This originated with the Capt who (tho' married) appears anxious to secure the hearts of some of them. And while this has set all the unmarried people by the ears, with the Skipper at their head, an equally trivial matter has created a quarrel between the two married Gents.[*] And the

---

[*] Samuel Alexander and Arthur Nicholson.

consequences are that the civilities of the table are performed coldly and silently—that there is a great saving of brandy and wine, and much less annoyance from their boisterous mirth and loose conduct than we were before troubled with.

Nor is the advantage altogether confined to the small portion of us who were unable to take a share in, and were disgusted with, their practices. But it has made them more resemble rational creatures than they did. I was not surprised at it as it is only the invariable consequence of conduct such as theirs. It was rather amusing to hear them upbraiding each other.

I slept on deck two nights. But as I did not relish the plan of all types and grades sleeping in our mess, without distinction, which plan our Capt was disposed to encourage, I have taken myself below.

18 January 1839. Friday

Lat: 13° 13' S. A good breeze and the Ship going her course—all well.

On revising a previous part of my journal I find that my first impressions of my fellow Voyagers were different from what they are now. This re-teaches me the lesson I have often learned, viz—that first impressions are usually wrong.

19 January 1839. Saturday

Lat: 16° S. Lon: 34°. Thermometer 85. It is only now that the fever of excitement has left me, caused by an unfortunate event on board our Ship. This is no less than a mutiny among the Sailors.

They had been guilty from time to time of sundry acts of petty theft, and last night about 5 oClock while the Capt was at dinner on the poop, one of them came aft and stole a bottle of porter out of a cask into which it had been stowed after being drafted off from a barrel. The cask was standing open opposite the main mast. I was sitting reading on the quarter deck at the moment and my attention was called to the Capt who had, on looking accidently round, detected him in the act.

The Capt ordered him aft. He refused to come and the Capt sprang from the poop and stood before him, so as to prevent him from escaping to the forecastle, while he ordered the third mate to take him aft by force. The Culprit struck the mate and also the Capt, and then the second mate. He was removed to the poop and, on their endeavouring to put him in irons, he resisted and called to his shipmates, who came and also opposed his being put in irons. The Capt let him go free from irons, but detained the prisoner, while the others went forward.

The Capt then, having spoken with the passengers, who were all disposed to give him every assistance, called the Sailors aft and asked them what they meant by opposing him in the execution of his duty and said that he would punish the prisoner and also every one of them for mutiny, and that it was his intention to put into Rio Janeira for that purpose.

One of them, who had been the ringleader all along, said that they were all equally guilty, and that they were all determined to oppose his authority. They however did not seem very unanimous. They then proposed still to work the Ship into Rio but some of them objected to this, and on then consulting among themselves they all said that they would not lift a hand so long as their comrade was detained a prisoner.

The Ships head was directed to Rio and the Capt, presenting a cocked pistol, told them that if one of them dared to come abaft the main mast, either to release the prisoner or for any other purpose, that moment should be his last. One or two of the fellows, baring their breasts, presented them and called 'fire', at the same time showing a disposition to cross the line, but were restrained by their comrades, while the first mate, presenting a drawn cutlass to the prisoner, dared him to move.

The Sailors, uttering many oaths and threats of vengeance, went forward. But who can describe the scene of terror depicted on every countenance. The women who were on deck at the first encounter shrieked and were sent below, which only increased their terror.

Almost every passenger on board volunteered their services to the Capt. A few were selected to keep the watches—all the firearms were carried into the Cabin and loaded. The pistols were loaded too—indeed I think if the mutineers had ventured any violent measures they must have been warmly received.

I was desired by the Capt to load my pistols. I put balls into a brace and laid them under my pillow, and also a double barrelled fowling piece along side my bed—and every person did the same. Night came on and every person watched, indeed sleep seemed to be banished for one night. All was quiet till about 11 oClock that I went to bed and lay down with my arms as I have described. I fell asleep and awaked again about 4 oClock—all remained quiet.

So anxious is every person to lend a hand that every thing was done this morning even before the usual time—decks washed and at this moment the Ship is sailing under every inch of canvas, altho' all her sails, but her main sails, had been stowed during the night. The passengers are divided into watches and they seem so expert that I am convinced they could take the Ship to her destination independently of the Sailors. We have a fair wind to Rio Janeira

and shall get there in about 4 days, when this matter
will be disposed of.

In regard to myself it is an adventure such as
I should not like to have every day, altho I do not
apprehend further danger as the Seamen—10 in
number—must see themselves too far outnumbered
to attempt any violence. Altho I do think that they
would stop at nothing that their power would effect
and it will prove a detention of the Ship for a time,
and lengthen the voyage and there will be some
witnessing &c &c. But I must just take my fate, which
of course will just be that of any other person in
the same circumstances. Well, I have seen a mutiny
on board a ship and slept with pistols loaded under
my pillow as a protection—I little dreamed of this
3 months ago.

I have given a brief outline of the matter, but of
course it falls short of giving a view of the reality,
which I am sure was sufficiently tragic. As to the
Capt I am convinced that he has acted quite right
in the present circumstances. But still I must say
that I am of opinion that if his command had been
more grave, and free from that sort of trifling levity
which characterises him, his Seamen would have
feared and respected him more and the present
unfortunate occurrence probably prevented. He was
always however kind to the Sailors many of whom
are very bad.

Some of the more devout on board are saying no better cd be expected on account of the wickedness of the people on board since we sailed.

20 January 1839. Sunday

Matters remain as they were last night. A complete plan of defence was adopted, sentinels posted, every weapon of defence put in requisition, so much care in short taken that if the mutineers had ventured an attack they must have rushed on their own destruction.

About 10 oClock at night they asked to speak with the Capt, and would have compromised if possible, but were informed that they had no excuse, and were told that there was no alternative but they must take their trials. That it could be proved they had said the Capt shd never see England in safety again—that it was evident to all that their intention was to make themselves masters of the ship by foul means—that the passengers did not consider themselves safe while they remained on board—that our measures had been taken, to defend ourselves by force of arms, if necessary—that the Capt was apprehensive of his personal safety, and they would be delivered up to justice as soon as we reached Rio de Janeira, to which place we were steering, and would reach in a very few days—that the Ship was wrought very well by the Emigrants, and no inconvenience felt by the want of them.

The Sailors—two or three of them, who were in my opinion only led by the others and did not know what they were doing till they found themselves caught—pleaded hard but without effect. They all denied that they had any evil intentions, and that their desire to speak with the Capt was to assure him of this.

They were then ordered forward—and were overheard uttering such resolves and threats as shewed that we had need of the greatest vigilance. The Capt, who overheard them himself, considered an attack certain before morning, now that they saw no prospect of pardon.

The sentinels were posted with increased care but every person on board stood sentry, and so strictly was the watch kept that McLean with true highland spirit challenged a pig which had got adrift 'to stand' while he presented his pistol and drew his cutlass. Poor grumpling was glad to retire to his sty, and McLeans promptitude and spirit have raised him in the estimation of all of us.

I and Mr Elphick waked all night ready for action. We have no regular watches altho' every person on board has, except ourselves. The Cabin Passengers watch by turn in the Cabin. Our precautions however were unnecessary as no hostilities took place and all is quiet to day. We have a beautiful breeze and are straight for Rio de Janeira, which we shall reach in a day or two.

Lat: 18° S. No divine service to day.

21 January 1839. Monday

All is still quiet. Guards were posted as carefully as ever last night. Beautiful breeze to day and we shall soon make Rio.

Sun northernwards to day at 12 oClock. I feel fatigued, having had little sleep and sundry starts at sounds real and imaginary these 3 nights past.

22 January 1839. Tuesday

Still in the same position. Wind favourable for Rio, which we are fast approaching.

Last night about 8 we had a squall from the westward, and two of the most vivid flashes of lightning I ever saw. It was exceedingly dark and gloomy and a trial for the nerves of our volunteer sailors and guards. They however remained firm and clued up* the small sails in good style. It passed in about an hour with a fall of rain.

---

* *Clue* is more usually spelt *clew*. It means to raise the lower corners of a square sail by means of clew lines.

To day we have a good breeze which sunk towards evening. The Capt was however anxious to try the volunteers at reefing topsails, and about 6 oClock ordered a reef.* All was made ready, and it was astonishing to see with what eagerness they scrambled up the shrouds, and ventured out on the yard arms† and very soon were the sails reefed by people who never were further than the deck before; all came down safely and proud of their feat and it has served as a subject to talk about since.

A sail seen to windward to day, steering our course. I was the first to see it from the yards.

23 January 1839. Wednesday

Calm. Watch and wind by night and trim sails &c by day. We are making no progress to day and it is exceedingly hot.

I have been thinking of beginning to write letters to leave at Rio—one for C.P. and one to P. Graham, to be read by him and other friends in London and then to be sent to Scotland. But tho' I have neither to

---

* A reef is that part of a sail which is taken in or let out by means of the reef points, in order to adapt the size of the sail to the force of the wind.
† A yard is a long tapering spar slung usually at right angles to a mast to support and spread the head of a square sail. Either end of the yard is called the yard arm.

watch nor trim sails nor anything else, it is so hot & oppressive that the task is almost more than I can accomplish. My friends will be astonished to hear of a mutiny on board the 'Planter'.

24 January 1839. Thursday

A dead calm to day and very rainy. The atmosphere is very close and we in vain look for a breeze. The volunteers don't much like watches by night while it rains so hard—and begin to flag.

25 January 1839. Friday

A light breeze to day and we make a little progress. All quiet with the sailors as yet. About 12 oClock noon we saw a sail to windward steering our course. We hove to with the intention of speaking her—she came up and proved to be a fine Norwegian barque bound to Rio Janeiro. Her reckoning was 2½ deg. more westerly than ours, and the event proved which of us was to be trusted. She passed to leeward of us and ultimately fell astern. Our Capt, confident in his own reckoning, kept steering to the westward.

26 January 1839. Saturday

I was aroused from a light sleep this morning about 1 oClock by all hands being called on deck to put the ship about, as she was almost aground.

I sprang up and ran on deck and found that it was too true. The breakers were dashing against the coast of Brazil with a sound of thunder. I saw them foaming, and the ship almost among them—she was not more than a cable's length from them. The Capt had kept going on with all sail set until he had almost caused the loss of the Ship and all on board, as he had no suspicion there was land so near.

Fortunately however it did not blow hard and on being put about she came off, and thus we narrowly escaped destruction. The Capt says that had she been 10 minutes longer in the same course no power on earth cd have saved us. The matter was so sudden that no person knew the danger we were in so the scene that must have taken place was prevented.

We are quiet off shore this morning, but our Capt & officers seem much at a loss to know what course to steer. We see the outline of the coast, which appears very irregular—sometimes on a level with the water, sometimes rising in high bluff peaks. They are looking for a high peak called the sugar loaf which marks the entrance to the harbour of Rio Janeiro.

I cannot look back upon the narrow escape we have had from shipwreck, perhaps from death, without gratitude to the Almighty preserver of all things for his preservation of men. I must say that the conduct of the Capt for carelessness and ignorance cannot be too much censured—and I apprehend yet further dangers as the consequence of it.

Calm to day and without motion. The Sea is changed to a deep dusky green, and shell fish and waterfowl in abundance.

27 January 1839. Sunday

A breeze in the morning, which sunk during the day and left us calm. We are near the coast of Brazil still, which is lovely beyond description—at every mile a beautiful peak rises in almost a perfect cone, and that again overtopped by another beyond on whose lofty summit rest eternal mists. I would never tire of looking at such a scene, and I could almost wish to climb every mountain and cast anchor in every bay.

About 7 p.m. a Steamer passed us, from which we learned that we were 32 miles from Rio. She was the 'Diana' of Liverpool and had been out 28 days only, while we have been twice as many—what a splendid mode of travelling this is. I hope it will be extended ere long to S. Australia.

Much thunder and rain tonight, lightning very vivid. We passed Cape Frio about 12 oClock noon. There is a lighthouse upon it. It is very high and abrupt.

28 January 1839. Monday

We had proceeded a little during the night and this morning got a view of the 'Sugar Loaf' at the entrance of the harbour of 'Rio de Janeiro'. It is a complete cone rising to a great height, very barren and inaccessible on every side. A Sea breeze sprang up at 12 oClock and we got slowly into harbour. There is a Land breeze till 12—then a sea breeze till Sunset.

I cannot possibly give any idea of the beauty of this coast, it is so lovely indeed and romantic—peak after peak rising in endless succession. The sky for part of the day unclouded—all nature clothed in eternal green. All captivate the sight and delight the fancy.

As soon as we had entered, a person with a speaking trumpet from a ship stationed at the entrance directed us to cast anchor, and afterwards put off in a boat and took a note of the ships name &c. He was a European—spoke English and lolled in the stern of his boat smoking a cigar.

Next 3 boats with flags came along side. One from the Custom house, a Portuguese Man of War—One from the British Consul and one from an English

Ship Chandler. I was much amused by the appearance of the fellows in their beautiful boats, lolling under an awning smoking, while the poor negro slaves were toiling at the oar. What I have seen of Rio is very charming—I have not yet gone ashore, but will in the morning and spend a day or so while the Ship remains.

The Capt boarded a Man of War and lodged his charge against the Sailors. Three of them who appear to have no hand of the matter and had been blindfolded by the cunning of the others will be punished and taken into the Man of War to serve a certain time.

It rains very hard tonight again. It is the rainy season here.

29 January 1839. Tuesday

Went on shore at Rio Janeiro this morning in company with Mr & Mrs Elphick—were rowed by slaves. Ordered some small necessaries to be sent on board, and then walked thro the town. Fox & Co. Englishmen supply provisions to the Ship. Dined at a French Hotel and afterwards took a boat to the Emperor's gardens.* Had a very pleasant sail about

---

* In 1839 Brazil was ruled by Emperor Pedro II. When the monarchy was overthrown in 1889 the Emperor's former

3 miles up the bay, then walked about 1 mile, and then entered the gardens. The boatman could speak English and interpreted every thing to us.

These gardens lie in a plain or prairie surrounded by high hills. They are of considerable extent and filled with every species of fruit trees. The vegetation is very rank, and rapid, and tho' a gang of slaves are continually at work, the order is much inferior to that of an English garden. It is laid out in squares and walks bordered by the coffee tree, which rises about 4 feet and was loaded with berries. The trees were loaded with fruit—oranges, lemons &c &c. Indeed we had just lighted on the spot when we saw at once all the fruit trees of the climate congregated—and enjoyed the shade of our orange grove very much.

It was very warm and fatiguing, and tho we walked slowly got dreadfully fatigued. We got all stung with mosquitos. It was very painful. Returned to the City and, having purchased some fruit, came on board.

Rio Janeiro is built on a bay the finest in the world. It is yet in a measure rude. The Streets are narrow and ill paved. The houses not tastefully finished and the grounds about them broken and unpolished. No extent of the town can be seen at once as it is built among very hilly ground along the coast, and high

---

gardens became a vast public park in which the Rio de Janeiro zoo is now housed.

peaks intervene. It is confined on the other side by very high hills which rise into peaks of great height.

There are a good many very decent stores, and substantial people—but the gentry are living in great numbers on the opposite side of the bay. Steamers go across every hour.

I was much struck with the appearance of the Slaves. All tribes and kinds. They carry immense burdens, and go in gangs of 10 or 12 when engaged in carrying a quantity of goods to or from a ship, and then they carry a great load on their heads, and trot along while they utter a peculiar sort of cry of encouragement, and one makes a sound with a rattle or bell. They are almost naked.

Some of the women who sell fruit in the streets are very gaily dressed, loaded with beads and baubles. There are no oxen used in carrying burdens, at least very few, and horses are apparently very scarce, and not good. The mules are very good, but a carriage drawn by two with a black fellow for postilion, with long whip, spurs and boots, is as amusing a spectacle as ever I saw. This however is the only equipage here, and a person who has never seen it cannot conceive what a figure it makes.

There are several convents here. I cannot like the *Nuns*.

In the evening I finished two letters to home. One to Mr P. Graham and one to C.P. Wrote very late and felt much fatigued.

30 January 1839. Wednesday

Went on shore about 10 oClock. Put my letters in the Post office. Walked about for several hours—very hot. Had some dinner—then took a boat to the other side of the harbour. Just as we stepped ashore a dreadful thunder storm broke on the bay, accompanied with a gale of wind, of great violence. One boat was sunk and another barge was driven ashore. The 'Planter' driven from her anchors almost a mile and a large ship alongside almost 2 miles. It was over in an hour and serene.

This is the most pleasant side of the harbour. The houses are neater and the place in better order. As Mr E. & I walked along the shore in front of the houses we were rather an object of curiosity to the swarthy citizens. The dark eyed beauties were just enjoying the coolness of the air after the storm, and we had an opportunity of seeing them. Tho' swarthy, they have an expression and softness in their large black eyes that makes their countenances very pleasing—and some I saw might be called pretty. After walking about a short time we were rowed on board.

31 January 1839. Thursday

Went again on shore this afternoon and walked about
a short time.

1 February 1839. Friday

A round of cannon was fired this morning from a
frigate in the harbour and from a fort. In the evening
there is a grand illumination of one of the churches.
It is a holiday among the Brazilians.

The Capt has been dreadfully gulled by the Agents
who supply the Ship with provisions. They have
charged exorbitant prices and asked 30% Ct* on a Bill
for the price. Their name is Fox & Co. Englishmen.

I had been on board all day stowing away fruit
&c as my stores and overhauling my Cabin so as to
start again with comfort. I have got 60 oranges, very
large and good, for almost nothing and other articles
very moderate.

2 February 1839. Saturday— Candlemas

The heat to day is very intense. We have got five
Sailors—One Arab, 2 Malays, one native of Bombay

---

* This possibly means 30 per cent on account.

and one of Bengal. Their manners are very curious and their speech more so. We have ½ doz English Sailors besides. We sail again tomorrow morning. I am satisfied of this place. Altho if I had plenty of time and money to spend I could like to spend a month here.

3 February 1839. Sunday

We were to have sailed this morning, but when the anchor was about to be heaved two of our Lascars[*] were awanting. They had been allowed to go ashore yesterday, and had not returned. A party were sent in search, but returned too late to sail this day, as it becomes very calm about 9 oClock and about 12 the Sea breeze sets in.

Yesterday various parties went over to the east side of the harbour, and used the private property of the people as if it had been their own. Went into vineyards and orange groves, broke trees &c &c. The Brazilians at length rose in a body and had well nigh 'served them out'. They however got off hot.

In returning to the Ship one of the boats which had been out of the water a long time leaked, and

---

[*] The word *Lascar* was most often used to describe sailors who originated from the Indian subcontinent. Often it specifically meant Muslim sailors from this region and that appears to be the case here, given the reference on 10 February.

being very heavily loaded was soon nearly full. They had to leave off rowing and bale out water with hats, caps &c. She drifted almost out of the harbour but fortunately a man of war's boat fell in with her and lightened her load, took her in tow and brought them on board with no further injury than a fright and wetting.

The most of them were tipsy, some of the women completely so. The mate was at the head of this party, which consisted of a part of the young women. The Capt took a number of them, and kept them on shore, till midnight. I could not consider myself in respectable company if I joined either party so I staid at home.

There is nothing but rioting and hubbub on board to day, and with the heat of the sun makes it quite intolerable.

4 February 1839. Monday

We expected to have sailed this morning without fail, but just as the Ship was getting under weigh, an officer came on board and on looking at our passports found only 17 passengers in it. He refused to clear the vessel, and here we are stuck for another day.

Such stupidity on the part of the Capt is insufferable, and makes him out an egregious blockhead indeed. He had on entering the harbour a paper given him containing full directions as to the place. Yet after remaining here three times as long as he had any need to do, he had by his stupidity thrown us, it may be, two or three days longer to roast beneath a vertical sun. He went ashore again last night with a party of the young women and returned late. If Brazilians had committed the same excesses in any part of England that some of our people have down here, they would soon have peopled our prisons and troubled our Magistrates.

The people do not work in the open air during the heat of the day but, as soon as the Sea breeze sets in, they sally out either for business or pleasure. They are very fond of music and perform well. The Ladies are to be seen only in the evening. The poor slaves are a very disagreeable spectacle and, when they are perspiring much, they have a very offensive smell. 'Oh Slavery! disguise thyself as thou wilt still thou art a bitter draught.'* I learn that the importation of Slaves is prohibited now but still they are smuggled and bought and sold privately. An English frigate lying in this harbour has two prizes—Slavers that

---

* The accurate quote is as follows: '"Disguise thyself as thou wilt, still, Slavery," said I, "still thou art a bitter draught."' It is from the novel *A Sentimental Journey Through France and Italy* by the Irish novelist Laurence Sterne, published in the year of his death, 1768.

she has taken with slaves on board. She is going to proceed with them to the West Indies.

A Frigate is a beautiful spectacle. Morals here still in retrograde motion on board the 'Planter'.

5 February 1839. Tuesday

Still disappointed in sailing to day. There was not a breath of wind in the morning and the heat was intense. The Sea breeze set in pretty early which relieved us from 138 degrees of heat in the sun. The evening was cool and a shower of rain fell which was very refreshing.

6 February 1839. Wednesday

This morning we have weighed anchor and got out of harbour. An officer came on board and gave us a password to carry us past the fort.

So farewell to Rio Janeiro. Farewell to this land of Slavery and despotism which defile as interesting a Country as ever lay to the Sun. Farewell to her darkeyed beauties whose mild features delight the fancy and lead captive the heart. If ever I return to England again it shall be my endeavour to spend a month at Rio de Janeiro.

Now for the wide Sea and the noisy waves again.

7 February 1839. Thursday

Last evening we had the grandest thunder storm I have ever yet seen. The lightning was very vivid and in such quantity as to light up the heavens all around for a second or so, then all was involved in pitchy darkness, and the thunder rolled and hurtled thro the air, and the rain fell in torrents. It lasted for 5 or 6 hours. Fortunately there was little wind, tho' that little blew from the Sea, otherwise we might have been in considerable danger as we were close in shore. This morning it is completely calm, and we lie in full sight of the bold and rugged coast of Brazil with its misty mountains and lofty peaks.

A slight breeze in the evening—and we make a little way. Saw the light on Cape Frio in the evening.

Several cases of sickness on board, the consequence of our visit to Rio Janeiro. The people one and all ate and drank there very immoderately and, now that they have got to Sea again, many of them have been very sick indeed. One of the Sailors (a pardoned one) was brought to the Ships side in a boat from the shore, hauled up with a rope's end, and has made a narrow escape from death by sickness since.

But I do not think the climate of Brazil very injurious to the health of a European. It must require care but, with an ordinary degree of attention to health,

I think it quite probable that a temperate person would reach a very old age. It is very hot during the morning till the sea breeze sets in; but it is then quite delightful, and the houses are so constructed that there is always a current of air passing thro them. But in this, as in all hot climates, temperance in every thing must be the best preservative of health.

8 February 1839. Friday

Calm; but a tremendous swell which makes the Ship roll dreadfully. Cape Frio in sight still.

A dolphin caught to day. Was a spectator of the various colours it assumes when dying, of which I had frequently heard. Spoke the 'Phoenix' of Jersey bound to Rio de Janeiro. She is a very smart little Brig.

Breeze from the Sea in the evening and we make a little—but I am afraid that it will take 3 more months to bring us to Australia.

9 February 1839. Saturday

Light breeze this morning which increases during the day. Quite out of sight of land to day. Heat is again gradually decreasing.

10 February 1839. Sunday

Fresh breeze this morning and the 'Planter' again breasts the wave. I have many thoughts about absent friends this morning as usual. Twice during the past week while my senses were steeped in deep sleep has my fancy led me to them—but when I awoke it was but a dream.

There has been no divine service on board for 3 Sundays now. Our people seem to have no heart to it. It is different with the Lascars. No morning passes without their offering up their devotions to their God who is no God. How then, oh you who call yourselves Christians—but who never by word or deed confess him to be your God, or acknowledge his power—will you answer to the living and true God?

The manners of these Lascars are very curious. They wear loose flowing dresses of showy colours, and bind a gay coloured handkerchief round their head and 2 of the same round their waist. When they choose to be in complete dress they use a silk umbrella and look very gaudy indeed. Their food is rice and fish, the latter of which with pickles they make into curry and then mix all together. When their food is ready they spread a mat and, placing the large dish in the middle, they sit round and eat it with their fingers. All their meals are the same. The Malay is not allowed to eat with the rest—his food is portioned out to him and he takes it by himself. They are very careful not to do anything unbecoming their 'Caste'. They refuse to use a broom and can't endure the sight of a pig, and when rallied about it, they say they would sooner cut their throats than touch one. Their language is dreadful jargon and, in common with all coloured tribes, they use a great deal of gesture in speaking.

11 February 1839. Monday

Fresh breeze to day and cloudy. Squally in the afternoon and evening.

The two principal authorities on board, viz Capt & Surgeon, have fallen out to day; indeed the Capt and the whole of the passengers are at variance, so much so that he has declined dining with them for some days. The little *drama* now draws to a conclusion and I suppose a few more acts will finish it—I mean our voyage, which well deserves the name of a drama.

12 February 1839. Tuesday

Calm or nearly so this morning and the wind rather unfavourable, which throws us rather out of our course.

There is a great difference of Climate now. The heat, even during the day, is not unpleasant and the evenings delightful. I have a slight headache to day, which prevents me from scribbling more.

13 February 1839. Wednesday

Strong breezes this morning, which increased during the day until we had too much of it to be pleasant— very heavy sea and the Ship pitched very heavily. Wind unfavourable and we have been hard to wind with close reefed topsails since midday. It blows harder to day than I have ever yet seen it. Very dark at night and boisterous.

14 February 1839. Thursday

Breeze to day. Still very fresh but a little more favourable. Put Ship about at 8 a.m. and she now lies within 2 points of her course.

Our voyage now must necessarily be a very long one indeed, and the Ships provisions are now very bad. I do not however require many of them, having laid in a small stock for myself at Rio Janeiro, having found it impossible almost to use many of the articles on board from their bad quality. I feel better to day than I have done this week before.

A Voyage to Australia

15 February 1839. Friday

Lat: 27° 18' S, Lon: 37° 40' W. Fresh breeze to day but unfavourable, increased towards evening when they reefed topsails.

My resources to expel 'ennui' are now scarcely sufficient to prevent me from experiencing that enemy in all his terrors. If we go on southwards as at present, without any easting, we shall soon get into winter again and just be Antipodes to those in England, who are now freezing over a coal fire while I am opening my bosom to admit the genial breeze. But they are in possession of many comforts to counter all this inconvenience—they are in the possession of friends and relations, and surrounded by ties which are all that render life desirable.

> But me, not destin'd such delights to share,
> My prime of life in wand'ring spent, and care:
> Impell'd, with steps unceasing to pursue
> Some fleeting good that mocks me with the view;
> That, like the circle bounding earth and skies,
> Allures from far, yet as I follow flies;
> My fortune leads to traverse realms alone,
> And find no spot of all the world my own.*

---

* These lines are from Goldsmith's *The Traveller*.

It is too soon for me to adopt these lines in their full meaning, but perhaps I may experience them in their fullest acceptation before I again see those who are now so far separated from me.

16 February 1839. Saturday

It blows still fresh this morning with a heavy head Sea, and in a direction very unfavourable for us. It is however carrying us Southwards very fast and we must just look for easting afterwards. Planets shone with remarkable brightness last night and the galaxy was very bright.

17 February 1839. Sunday

Lat: 32° 11' S, Lon: 35° 15' W. Wind changed this morning. It is now very favourable, and away we go at 6 to 7 miles an hour. The motion of the Ship lurching and pitching so much is very unpleasant, but the knowledge that we are going forward on our voyage makes it easily endured.

There is no acknowledgement of God on board this morning—I suppose it is very convenient for our authorities to forget that such a being exists, but a time will come when they will have leisure to repent when it may be too late.

An unfortunate female fell down the main hatchway last evening and broke her leg. She is one of the 16 young women we have on board (though not young). She may be about 40 and has been no doubt a balladsinger. By her loose conduct among the sailors, and noisy, coarse and disgusting talk, joined to a very unprepossessing personal appearance, she had become obnoxious to almost every one, and went under the soubriquet of 'Old Gallows'.

Her real name is Lizzy Taylor* and it was with a kind of triumph that some heard of her misfortune, that appeared in my eyes no less than savage. She has no friends nor acquaintances on board, and it wd be difficult to say what object she can have in going to S. Australia, but still more so what object the Comrs can have in granting such a creature a free passage.

Our 'juvenile Sawbones' has bound her leg with a piece of ropeyarn, but God knows what will become of this wretched creature.

---

* Lizzy Taylor was a domestic servant from Greenwich, who in fact appears to have applied for free passage at the same time as another domestic servant from Greenwich named Eliza Smith, so she must have had one friend on board. Taylor gave her age as 29 in 1838.

18 February 1839. Monday

Wind blows fresh this morning but very favourable indeed. We have got the breeze on our quarter, and away she jumps splendidly—8 to 10 miles an hour. This will make up for lost time—but it seems necessary to call at Tristan da Cunha nevertheless, which will not expedite us much.

The mornings and evenings now are pretty cold and it is very agreeably cool during the day.

At 7 oClock in the evening we had the most tremendous squall I have ever yet seen. It had begun to rain with high wind about 4, and had continued to blow pretty fresh, but at last it became gloomy and pitchy dark to windward and suddenly broke upon us in awful fury. At first it blew steadily and the ship dashed along with amazing velocity, but at last it began to waver and shake our sails, which put us in no small danger of having our masts carried away or being thrown on our beam ends before the sails could be trimmed. It however as suddenly died away and all was got to rights.

The appearance of the Sea was grand beyond description and the fury of the waves appalled the most daring.

We have had a squall of another kind between the Capt and Cabin Passengers about the food. The Capt boards[*] them all himself at a certain price agreed on by the owners. During the first part of the voyage, while a cordial feeling prevailed between them and the Capt, they fared well. But now that he looks more to his own interest, they feel a difference, and have made a regular *row* about it. The consequence will add nothing to their comfort.

At 9 oClock still squally and uncomfortable.

19 February 1839. Tuesday

It has rained excessively all night with alternate squalls and calms, and this morning we have a pretty steady breeze and favourable. But the rain still pours in torrents and renders it very gloomy and unpleasant as the companions[†] are covered over, and the rain makes us all prisoners below. I have never seen it rain with such fury in Scotland. It appears as if 'Wide-rent . . . the clouds Pour on a whole flood'.[‡]

The Capt informs me this morning (unasked) that the Passengers ask a bottle of wine each, per day[§]

---

[*] One of the older meanings of *board* is to provide food in exchange for a payment, as in the phrase *board and lodgings*.

[†] On a boat, the companion is a skylight or window frame that allows light into the lower decks.

[‡] These words come from one of James Bell's favourite poems, Thomson's *The Seasons: Summer*.

[§] A bottle a day was more than the stipulated amount of a pint a day, set out by the Commissioners. In this instance the

viz 1 pint Port and 1 pint Sherry, besides Porter &
Brandy. This appears to me more than any sober
person should drink and certainly more than any
respectable person would drink.

The Ship however is consigned to Mr McLaren,
the S. Australian Co. manager at Adelaide, who is
from all accounts a good & pious man*; and who
will know exactly what wine ought to be drunk
per day—and in my opinion the Capt has little to
fear. They have no specific rate of provisions agreed
on. The transaction was considered to be among
gentlemen, and they expected to be treated as such
and in my opinion have been so treated; but perhaps
more so before, as I have before mentioned, some
unpleasant circumstances caused a variance among
them. And it is as well for a good many of them that
their desires are a little under restraint from outward
circumstances, as they appear to have little power
over them themselves.

I have been reading Dr Franklin's maxims on
frugality and economy†, and have made resolution
to adopt a good many of them.

---

cabin passengers seem to have had an alternate 'gentleman's
agreement' with the captain.
* David McLaren, Angas's manager in Adelaide, was known
as a strict Scotch Baptist Calvinist.
† In 1807 the London publishers Dayton and Harvey had issued
a version of Benjamin Franklin's American classic, *Poor*

20 February 1839. Wednesday

This morning it is calm, but with such a swell as I have never yet seen. The Ship rolls very heavily indeed, and we have had such a morning with casks, coops &c rolling about to the great danger of breaking legs, necks &c &c before they could be secured, and crockery of every description was crashing in every part of the Ship. These were at last secured, but the rolling increased towards evening and became so exceedingly great that it was with much difficulty I could make myself believe that the Laws of gravitation ensured the Ship from capsizing. As She again & again dipped her gunwales in the water, a shriek escaped from those whose nerves were least firm. While it was only by dint of holding hard that we were prevented from rolling overboard, between decks it was quite insufferable.

The Sea fell about 3 oClock on Thursday morning and a slight breeze sprang up which has a little relieved us from the most uncomfortable sensation I ever felt. However much I may dread a storm, it will henceforward yield me real pleasure compared with a calm in a swelling Sea.

Richard's Almanack, under the title *Maxims and Morals from Dr. Franklin: Being incitements to industry, frugality, and prudence.* It can be reasonably assumed it is to this high-minded volume that Bell is referring here.

A good many birds are flying about to day and among them the Cape Albatross. One was shot which measured 9½ feet from the tip of the one wing to the tip of the other.

21 February 1839. Thursday

Lat: 33° 32', Lon: 27° 24'. Very light breeze this morning and a slight swell. Nothing however compared with yesterday's, which was such as I hope I shall never again see. I have had very little sleep last night and feel fatigued. I trust we shall not be long in this latitude without a good wind.

22 February 1839. Friday

A pretty fresh breeze sprang up last evening with rain and fog. It continues to day at times raining, at others with a thick 'Scotch mist' which wets an 'Englishman to the skin' and a pretty good breeze, which however is unfavourable, as our steerage is south west instead of east.

We have now been nearly 3 months to Sea and a long voyage before us still—but thank God I feel my health and strength unimpaired. However I shall hail the moment with unspeakable joy that points to the time when I shall be freed from the intolerable annoyance to which I have been subjected on board.

It is not the danger of the Sea or any other thing connected with it that ought to alarm the Voyager to Australia—it is the coming in contact with people of low character and loose morals that will prove his misery and will outrage every feeling he possesses of a contrary description, and make him miserable indeed. And though his only plan will be, like mine, to separate himself as much as possible, yet he will be very much annoyed still.

23 February 1839. Saturday

Wind very favourable to day, having gradually veered round during yesterday and last night. It carries us about 5 miles an hour. Sky clear and brilliant. We have a new *Act* in our little *drama*. I shall relate it, as it will throw a good deal of light on the previous part of our voyage.

We have on board an old man who was called a Dr at the beginning of our voyage. It seems however he has been licensed to preach, but has always taught a school at Liverpool, from which place he is, and goes out to S. Australia having got a free passage with 11 daughters and 2 Sons. His name is McGowan—I think he says he has lived at Rock Ferry.*

---

* Rock Ferry is situated in England's Merseyside.

Well our Capt of course could not want a mistress till he returned to his own in England, but made love to 2 of McGowans daughters. They, silly enough, listened to him and, instead of being corrected by their father, were rather encouraged, as the whole family found their profit in it, in the way of sundry presents of wine, brandy, fresh provisions &c &c.* The Capt was allowed to keep the daughters company at all hours and, during the whole time of our being in warm weather, one bed on deck sufficed for all three, while at Rio he took them ashore and had the audacity to exhibit them there. The stupid old father winked at such ongoings—altho' in the opinion of every one on board the honour of his daughters was sacrificed to his neglect of his duty as their father, while his wife was equally deficient in hers.

As I have before hinted, such an example was soon followed up by all the Ships Co. But particularly the 3 Mates carried their immorality to a glaring height, particularly the 1st mate—whom I saw take farewell of a wife and child at Deptford, and who is a man of 40 or more. And it was quite common to see the Capt occupying the 3d part of the bed on deck, and the 3 mates sharing theirs with such ladies as esteemed it

---

* The Macgowans, travelling in steerage, would have welcomed the extra food and wine—no wine was provided to steerage travellers.

an honour worthy of their acceptance. And, thanks to the Colonization Comrs, they soon found many such, who seemed to like their Cabins so much better than their own part of the Ship, that they were found there by day as well as by night.

And they always found ample means of securing themselves under cover of a couple of beings, natives of some obscure Alley, in some obscure Street, of that renowned city London, and who are carrying in themselves all this filth of the place of their nativity to Adelaide, whither they are going to sell a quantity of goods of a quality that would outstrip those of the most 'subtle Isaac'* in all Christendom.

This worthy couple possess one descendant of about a years growth, who possesses a pair of pretty sound lungs and rarely forgets to give them play. Then this descendant must be nursed, and what so handy as this as an excuse for these Ladies being in our part of the Ship.

This went on for some time and, altho I at two separate times exposed such practices to the Capt and an end was put to it, still in two days it was equally bad. Indeed what could the Capt say when

---

* Possibly a reference to the 1833 novel *Tom Thornton* by the American lawyer-turned-politician Richard Henry Dana. The hero's wife is seduced by a Jew named Isaac who has embroiled the couple in crippling financial debt. Eventually Thornton kills Isaac.

his own conduct was so much the same. But 'a time for every thing' as the wise man says. This went on so long as our Capt & Surgeon were 'hand in glove' but when each of them had an account to settle with the other, and a personal pique to gratify, the state of things was altered and the Dr first complained to the Capt of the conduct of his officers. This compelled the Capt to take measures to put an end to it, and accordingly he sent them a written intimation that, if such conduct was persevered in, it must be at the expense of their commissions. They answered him very insolently and he evidently feels himself in an awkward predicament as he has pocketed their insolence, which he wd be the last person to do if he knew that his own conduct would bear scrutiny.

He came to me to day and related these facts about the letters, with which however I was acquainted, and as usual made some story to conciliate me and make me believe that he had done his duty, which however he will not effect so long as I am able to judge of facts which pass before my eyes in a consistent manner.

I told him that his officers had indeed been conducting themselves in a scandalous manner, and that upon the whole the manner in which the Ship had been conducted would not bear scrutiny, to which it wd at some period be exposed, as certainly every thing connected with it would be made known in

London, and I advised him to look to himself, and his own interests.

He said that it was his intention to represent the conduct of these Girls to the Comrs resident in Australia, and the Master of one of them, by whom she was discarded on account of her conduct, intended to prosecute her for defamation of character on his arrival in the Colony. This is a Mr Alexander who with his wife are passengers on board and appear very respectable, and report makes them very rich. They have a number of Servants on board, and among them this Girl*, whom they have discarded, and whom they intend to prosecute on account of something she had said prejudicial to their character. However I am persuaded the Capt will keep all about the Voyage as quiet as possible, as he will dread an exposure of his own character.

Breeze towards evening rather decreased.

24 February 1839. Sunday

Dead calm this morning and all day. This day was ushered in by our gents on board shooting at Albatrosses, and in the afternoon they put to Sea in

---

* Probably Maria Lucas of Suffolk, whose application for a free passage gives 'S. Alexander' as her agent/sponsor.

a boat for the same purpose. The Sky is remarkably clear this morning, and the horizon very beautiful.

Boat returned in the evening with 3 Albatrosses, 1 Cape hen and 1 'Mother Carey's chicken'.* So much for the way in which this day has been spent.

The heavens were remarkably beautiful this evening—rendered more so by a very bright Moon and the Stars shining very bright.

25 February 1839. Monday

Lat: 35° 58', Lon: 23° 41'. Steady breeze this morning and fine weather. We make 4 to 5 miles an hour in our course—I hope it will continue and let us get forward a little.

I have been reading Cooks Voyages, I have not read them before, and am now a good deal entertained with the account of the Voyages of that great Navigator. I have not yet arrived at his lamentable death, which was such a Sacrifice to the cause of science and philosophy.

How much I wish that I knew how all gets on at home now among all my friends. But a long time must elapse before I can have any communication from them.

----

* One of the nicknames of the storm petrel is *Mother Carey's chicken*.

26 February 1839. Tuesday

Steady breeze this morning and fair. This is a very busy day on board—breaking out the hold, to allow the Emigrants to provide themselves with changes of clothes. Last time this was done, it was hoped it would not again be required; but our lengthened Voyage has rendered it again necessary.

People all well on board still and I hope we shall not have any disease before we land. We expect to make Tristan da Cunha in a few days and will again be gratified with a sight of Land. It is rather cold now, and obliges me to wear thick clothing. I have caught a slight cold from it, which affects my head a great deal.

27 February 1839. Wednesday

Lat: 35° 24', Lon: 19° W. Fresh breeze sprang up last evening—and foul. It continues to day cloudy and unfavourable—carrying us southwards. It is now very evident how much time we have lost by turning into Rio, as there is not the least doubt that we would have reached Tristan da Cunha on 1st February or sooner, and now on the 1 March we are still a good many degrees from it, thus leaving us for another month upon the Sea. Still great numbers of Albatrosses and other birds flying about.

28 February 1839. Thursday

Fresh breeze and favourable sprang up about midnight and had continued all day. We have of course made a little way on our long voyage.

It was discovered last night that the Masts and Yards were in a very bad state—and had been ever since we left London. The Capt was very angry and they have set about doing what they can to repair them, but still they must be in a very poor state indeed, and a long voyage before us. This is however just on a level with the general way in which the Ship has been prepared for Sea. And if we had had any hard weather we must have been in a poor condition before now. I cannot see how the Insurers can be liable for any damage sustained by a Vessel sent to Sea in such a state.

1 March 1839. Friday

It blows very hard to day with a very high Sea and waves rising to an amazing height. It is by far the roughest weather we have had yet, but it is clear and the sun shines.

By calculation last night, we were 80 miles from Tristan da Cunha, which we were expecting to see to day. But it has been discovered to day that by an error in the calculation, or thro wrong steerage, we are 120 miles from it on another course. This does not say much for our seamanship and we are now scudding south east with the wind on our quarter and the additional accommodation of a heavy Sea at intervals scraping the decks.

The Sea in a storm is a grand spectacle, but I think I would view it with more satisfaction if I were myself on *terra firma*, instead of being tossed about at the mercy of the winds and waves— knowing the frail state of the Ships rigging. The bottom however is very tight and she admits no water.

2 March 1839. Saturday

After a very stormy night and the Sea running mountains high, we have less wind to day but still a heavy Sea, and it is most piercing cold.

About 4 oClock last night our main topsail Yard broke with a crash, and it was found to be as rotten as could be. It was blowing very hard at the time. They had a spare yard which was rigged as soon as possible and the sail bent upon it, about 9 oClock at night. This is just a specimen of what we may expect of almost the whole rigging and masts of the Ship, and it gives me a good deal of annoyance to think that we are in such a stormy Sea in such a state.

We can see nothing of Tristan da Cunha yet, and it is thought that we must have passed it. If this is the case, I think in all probability we shall have to put into Table Bay at the Cape of Good Hope and refit. This will make our passage both dangerous and tedious. It is amazing to me how they cd have sent the Ship to Sea in such a state. I do however put my trust in God alone to bring me safe to end of my voyage. But if it is otherwise determined, I trust he will prepare me for all the appointments of his Providence concerning me.

I never till within the last two months experienced the blessedness of those who put their trust in God in the same degree that I have felt it. And it is a blessing, above every other, to be desired. To think that in the midst of every danger his arm is around you, and that you are in his care and keeping, disarms even death of all his terrors and makes a person prepared for encountering all the ills of life.

3 March 1839. Sunday

Yesterday at 12 oClock it was discovered that Tristan da Cunha had given us the slip, and that we had passed it. But from the quantity of Sea weed floating and the number of birds, it appeared as if land were at no great distance. It would have been a foolish task to have spent time in endeavouring to make it, so we stood to the East with a pretty fresh breeze right aft, which has caused the Vessel to roll a good deal.

It has been determined on to make Algoa Bay after doubling the Cape of Good Hope, and there refit and take in a supply of fresh provisions of which we stand in a good deal of need—besides many other necessaries of which the Ship stands much in want as she had been very inadequately provided at first.

To day we have a light breeze and clear weather. But by setting a good deal of sail we are making considerable progress on our Voyage, which is becoming rather a cruise round the world than anything else.

I left Europe 3 months ago and have visited America. In a short time I shall set my foot in Africa, and afterwards (God willing) shall proceed to Asia—thus having visited the 4 great divisions of our Globe. So much for my travels. People are busy to day making a new fore Yard—this is the first time I have seen ordinary work wrought on Sunday.

I think I may expect letters for me at Adelaide long before I reach it myself as several Vessels were about to sail soon after us.

4 March 1839. Monday

I was called up this morning to see a large porpoise which had been speared and hauled on board. He was an immense fellow and yielded a considerable quantity of oil. His carcase was cut up and distributed to all and sundry who would partake, and there was such a frying and roasting. Some compared it to beef steaks; some to one thing and some to another. I tasted it and compare it to nothing that I ever before tasted, but found it extremely disagreeable to my palate. It had a strong rancid taste, and smelled something like fish saturated in train oil.

We have a light breeze to day and cloudy dull weather, but from the rapidity of the current it seems that we sail without wind, as we are making a considerable Longitude every day.

Ship rolled a good deal during the night.

5 March 1839. Tuesday

Lat: 35° 12', Lon: 1° 57' W. Nearly calm this morning, and dull & cloudy.

We are now nearly deprived of the beautiful starlight nights we had within the tropics, that were so lovely I could frequently have looked on heavens during the whole night. The evenings are now dull and obscure.

There is a piece of poetry by Mr McDiarmid*, Editor of the Dumfries Courier, which I have many

---

* John McDiarmid was the owner and editor of the *Dumfries Courier*; he was also president of the local Burns Club and author of a number of books.

times admired, and have just to day by chance laid my hand upon it. It is a child's first impressions of a Star.

She had been told that God made all the stars
That twinkled up in heaven; and now she stood
Watching the coming of the twilight on,
As if it were a new and perfect world
And this were its first eve. How beautiful
Must be the work of nature to a child
In its first impression! Laura stood
By the low window, with the silken lash
Of her soft eye upraised, and her sweet mouth
Half parted, with the new and strange delight
Of beauty that she could not comprehend,
And had not seen before. The purple fold
Of the low sunset clouds, and the blue sky
That looked so still and delicate above,
Filled her young heart with gladness; & the eve
Stole on with its deep shadows. Laura still
Stood, looking at the West with that half smile
As if a pleasant thought were at her heart.
Presently in the edge of the last tints
Of Sunset, where the blue was melted in
To the faint golden mellowness—a star
Peeped suddenly. A laugh of wild delight
Burst from her lips, and putting up her hands

Her simple thoughts burst forth expressively
'Father, dear father! God has made a star.'

This is very beautiful, and gives the full expression of what the feelings of a child in the circumstances may be supposed to be.

The monster *Vice* still reigns supreme on board the 'Planter'.

6 March 1839. Wednesday

Pretty fair breeze this morning tho' cloudy, and we get on a little. Last evening we had another scene in our drama, in which I made my debut as, I believe, the principal Actor.

On account of certain differences in the Cabin, the Capt and a number of the Cabin Passengers found it impossible to carry on any of their cabals there, and fixed upon the intermediate Cabin as the next best place for their purpose. Of course it was thought necessary to ask our leave, which was due, accompanied by an invitation to join them in a sort of Club for drinking and smoking, from 8 to ½ past 10 oClock, on Tuesday and Friday evenings weekly. I said that for my own part I could not think that it would give me any annoyance, provided it was conducted with decorum and the proper hours observed; but that, as there were Ladies there as well as in the

Cabin of course, they would be most annoyed by it, and that I would not give my consent provided they were unwilling that it should take place. The *Jew* and his *Jewess* at once consented and Mr & Mrs Elphick, seeing that their dissent would not prevent it, did not offer any objections.

So of course the Meeting took place and was '*yclept*'* *the Welcome Club*. The glass and song went on and *operated*. Half past 10 came; another half hour was added on account of its being the first evening, and after that I saw that another half hour was still too short a time to dismiss the Meeting. The Doctor however had proposed a certain song by way of bringing the meeting to a close, but was disregarded.

At this time I considered it my duty to apprize the Club that the time of closing was come, and gone, and that Mr & Mrs Elphick were upon Deck—at that time of night, unable to join the Club and equally so to remain in their Cabin or return to rest. They had waited patiently till the hour fixed for closing the meeting had come and now, while we were enjoying ourselves below, we were doing them great injustice in exposing a female in the open air at such an hour. And of course her husband could take no part in the Club, being unable to leave his wife. I concluded by

---

* *Yclept* is a Middle English word, much loved by Chaucer. It means 'called'.

seconding the Doctor's motion of singing the song and dismissing the meeting.

This had the desired effect—the meeting was dismissed. But still it gave rise to a good deal of discussion, and several of them had to apologize to Mr & Mrs E. for the annoyance given them, and not a few of them were highly offended with me for my interference. To all such I gave a sufficient explanation to convince them that they had got into the wrong box when they attempted to enjoy themselves at our expense.

The Capt, though he had seen the matter in its true light at first, was impressed otherwise by some of the other Gents. I however declined discussing the matter with him publicly; but, taking him aside, I & Mr E. spoke to him freely what we thought on the subject, and other subjects at the same time. And I was glad to find that he possessed the same opinions as to the general state of matters as we did, tho' he had been induced by the others to act as he did. On concluding he was pleased to express a high opinion of my conduct particularly, which he had observed during the whole of the Voyage, and, after detailing some of his own grievances from the Passengers, he concluded by saying that he was sorry that he had been unable to study our comfort so much as he wished. He made many promises for the future, all of which we thanked him for, tho' well aware that we need not look for any fulfilment.

So I think that in all probability this will be the beginning and end of the Welcome Club. How much I do wish that we had reached the end of our voyage.

7 March 1839. Thursday

Fresh breeze this morning and we go on smoothly and pleasantly. In the afternoon we have an auction mart on board and it is surprising what numbers of articles are brought forward and bought eagerly.

There is also a newspaper established, which however is entirely devoted to satire and buffoonery which, tho' it may endure for a time & amuse, will be sure to end in something disagreeable. I have this evening sent a communication to its Editor, entreating him to change its character, or at least devote a portion of it to subjects of a scientific or literary nature, and have sent a specimen for insertion, and promised my contribution under the agnomen of 'Philomathos'* – at the same time showing the practicability of establishing a highly useful periodical. I hope I shall succeed in making it worthy of perusal, instead of being a lampoon on the character of individuals.

---

* That is, a lover of learning.

I had a conversation with the Dr Superintendant last night which I shall relate by & bye.

8 March 1839. Friday

Strong gale this morning and Sea runs very high. It increased during the day and blew very hard all night. It is also excessively cold and, after taking in all the sails except the main sails and double reefed topsails, we let the Ship run. The gale is from the SW and our course nearly East. We are making 8 miles an hour in a very heavy Sea and the Vessel lies almost on her side. Spent a sleepless night.

9 March 1839. Saturday

Gale increased to day and the Sea, which runs still higher, breaks over us very heavily, while the waves run with such fury that, as they break against her side, they give a shock which makes her whole timber crack. Shortened sail still further and held on our course. Feared a good deal for our yards and masts which are so frail. Tried the pumps. She makes no water.

10 March 1839. Sunday

Gale still on the increase with sudden squalls and rain. The Sea penetrates every seam of the decks and sides of the Ship, which from their having been high above the water have become relaxed. It penetrates all the Cabins and makes it very unpleasant, and dangerous to health as it is very cold & damp. We have been making very great progress however and will make Algoa Bay (God willing) in a few days.

The Sea is running amazingly high, and to one unaccustomed to it presents a grand, sublime and rather appalling spectacle. They are still shortening sail this evening.

I have had my usual thoughts of home to day. I have been thinking of the religious privileges I enjoyed and feel now, as I am sure I shall feel for long, that this is a loss more to be regretted than any other. But I console myself with the knowledge that God is to be found in the dwellings of Jacob as well as in the Gates of Zion.

Another Newspaper has appeared to day, and commences with my article to which special attention is drawn in the Editorial remarks. On the whole it is much superior to the last number.

11 March 1839. Monday

Gale continued to day. It blew harder than ever in the afternoon with a very heavy Sea.

At 12 noon we heaved the lead but found no soundings at 100 fathoms. We are now fast approaching the Cape and feel anxious as the nights are very dark and stormy. The day is however quite clear and with ordinary caution we ought to run in no danger, but I have never been able to put much confidence in our Seamen—and we may, as before, run ourselves in danger. Our Ship stands this hard weather well and she rides over these rough seas truly.

No day passes ever without a quarrel in some part of the Ship and we have always something unpleasant in agitation.

It is 9 oClock and I shall retire to rest and trust to God to bring me in safety to the light of another morning.

> Unless the Lord do build the house
> The builders lose their pain
> Unless the Lord do watch the house
> The watchmen watch in vain.*

---

* This is one version of a Presbyterian Psalter based on Psalm 127.

12 March 1839. Tuesday

This morning we had less wind and a smoother Sea, and sail along pleasantly.

We were keeping a sharp lookout for land, and about 10 oClock land was seen among the parting clouds—at last, top after top of high land broke upon the view until at length the Cape of Good Hope presented the usual delineaments belonging to it. These are a very high land called table mountain, to the right a peak called the sugar loaf, and in that same direction an abrupt termination called the Lion's rump. On the left it ends in an equally abrupt termination of the high land called the lions head, and then low land stretches northwards towards Saldanhah Bay.* As soon as it was ascertained that we were all right, we put about and stood away from land until we can make Algoa Bay and at midday we can scarcely distinguish the highest peak of the shore.

A schooner was beating her way into Table Bay† but we were not sufficiently near to speak her. It may

---

* Normally spelt Saldanha Bay, it is named after one of the earliest European explorers of this region, the Castilian Portuguese captain Antonio de Saldanha. It is on the south-western coast of South Africa, north-west of Cape Town.
† Table Bay is Cape Town's harbour.

be several days yet before we reach Algoa Bay* as the
wind is not very favourable.

I cannot describe the sensations of myself and all
on board on again seeing land. All my past fears and
trouble seemed to vanish in an instant. Joy sprang up
afresh in my bosom and I hailed the happy prospect
of finishing my voyage in safety. I returned thanks
to the giver of every good gift for his unspeakable
loving kindness.

13 March 1839. Wednesday

Last evening a strong breeze sprang up and put us
under close reefs. We had again stood in for land and
were running 7 or 8 knots an hour, when the man
who had just been placed at the mast head called out
'breakers on the lee bow'. A few minutes sufficed to
put her about, and we again stood off and continued
so all night. This morning early we stood in again,
but had the vexation to see the land again bearing
exactly the same as it did yesterday morning when
first seen, so that we had not gained a mile since. We
have continued standing off and on all day but have

---

* Algoa Bay is a wide inlet along South Africa's east coast,
almost 700 kilometres east of the Cape of Good Hope and
near modern-day Port Elizabeth. To reach it, of course, the
Planter needed to sail under the Cape.

made nothing, but I am happy to hear that the wind has shifted a little since sunset. It blows pretty fresh.

Last evening again the Club met and had their sitting on deck—not in our Cabin. They made a dreadful noise and kept up the same till a late hour this morning. I have cut the Club. The chief mate, whom I have mentioned before, got very drunk and his swearing was most profane; but I have seldom seen an instance of more immediate vengeance, on the part of that being whose name he had taken in vain. Scarcely had he laid himself down to sleep, which, as his berth was wet, he did upon a table, than he fell asleep. But it was of short duration—a heavy lurch of the Ship rolled him over and, as he is a heavy man, bloated with hard drinking, he fell with great violence and his head came in contact with the corner of our iron stove, which cut and mangled him most dreadfully.

I was the first to render him assistance and got a light and called the Surgeon, who had just left him a few minutes before, himself flushed with drinking. The wound was dressed and the poor fellow put to bed amidst great suffering, where, while he lies, may God turn his heart to a sense of his sinfulness—and may it prove a lesson to all of us.

But my having occasion to go on deck at that hour brought me to the knowledge of still more to give me uneasiness. I found the officer on watch asleep, and so drunk that I could not make him understand what had happened, and so left him to his sottishness. Upon me going to the man at the wheel, I found him an hour too late in being relieved, and unable to make the next man understand this was the case, as no bells had been struck. I took the helm till he roused the watch who, instead of being on deck, had taken their opportunity of going down to their hammocks. I did my best to get them rallied; but to think of such a state of things in a smart gale of wind, and we on a lee shore.

There is little appearance of our being able to weather the Cape, unless we get a change of wind and while we beat about so long we are protracting our voyage dreadfully. It blows from SE, which is rather extraordinary as all accounts agree in saying that NW winds prevail at this season. At all events it is a stormy place.

14 March 1839. Thursday

It blew very hard all night, and this morning particularly we had a very severe gale. It split every sail we could hoist, and left us at last hauled up with our foresails and these in a shattered state.

It calmed about midday but we find that we have been drifted a good deal to the south west and are altogether out of sight of land. We are however again standing in. No appearance still of a change of wind and we are losing, instead of gaining, ground.

Altho used now to high winds, I had a sleepless night and feel exhausted to day. Tomorrow we have a change of moon and eclipse of the Sun; but I hope we shall have what to us at present is of more consequence—a change of wind.

Sailors busy to day in unbending old sails and replacing them with new ones. At 4 p.m. saw land again; at 8 stood out again.

15 March 1839. Friday

Very Calm this morning and we are close in land. The coast tho beautiful presents none of those characteristics which render the coast of S. America so charming. It is apparently bare and heathlike. The elevations are moderate in height and not formed into peaks like the coast of Brazil. A range of lofty mountains however appear behind and bound the view. Table mountain bears a striking resemblance to that from which it derives its name, and it is remarkable that the Colonists can judge with the utmost certainty when a storm is approaching—from a white cloud which broods over the summit of this mountain, which is called the 'tablecloth'. It is spread by degrees until condensed to a certain degree, and then the storm breaks with dreadful fury, and after enduring for 24 hours or so the cloth is again withdrawn and the storm abates. It was after seeing this cloud that we had such a gale of wind. And no wonder that this should be a stormy place when we consider that all the fury of both the Indian and Atlantic oceans are here concentrated, and here expend their strength.

We have still to day no prospect of making round the Cape but still we feel grateful for such a pleasant day after such stormy weather. This part of the Sea is as muddy as the Thames at London and is covered with Sea weed and other vegetable substances driven from the shore. Also abundance of waterfowl and sharks. I saw also a very fine turtle which, on being disturbed, dived under water.

I think it probable if we do not get a fair wind soon we shall put into Table Bay.

No eclipse of the Sun visible here. It has shone bright all day.

16 March 1839. Saturday

Last night at Sunset a fresh breeze sprang up suddenly which increased to a smart gale during the night. We had been standing close in shore and sounding at intervals. After nearing land as close as was consistent with safety, we put about and stood out till midnight. We then stood in again and got in sight of land about

10 this morning, a little to leeward of what we were yesterday. Thus there is still no appearance of our getting round. It blows pretty fresh to day still and seems increasing. If we had had ordinary luck, we would have been in Adelaide.

17 March 1839. Sunday

This morning we have again stood in to land and as usual we have got in sight of land about midday, but have made no further progress in making round the Cape. There is a strong feeling of discontent springing up on board, and no little blame is imputed to the Capt. No doubt he is to blame, but he has brought upon himself consequences equally bad with any of us, as he is a great deal out of pocket, having to board the Cabin passengers so much longer—and I am afraid has done himself a good deal of injury otherwise.

When he resolved upon making Algoa Bay, he calculated on making land to the Eastward of the Cape; but from some cause or other to be attributed to himself, having I believe been out in his reckoning, we have made land northward of the Cape, the consequence of which is that here we are stuck as if the doors of the East were thrice locked against us—and day after day we have looked in vain for having made a little way Southward, but have been disappointed.

Altho' if we have stood far enough south when we had it in our power, we might have made Algoa Bay with as much ease as we have done this place.

Fresh provisions on board are completely exhausted, and to day they have killed a poor little goat brought by one of the passengers from Rio de Janeiro. In short I think we shall have to try Saldhana Bay unless we have a change of wind soon, of which there is no present appearance. Table Bay we could make but, as the Ship is insured and premium paid on the condition that she would not go near the Cape of Good Hope, of course if we put into Table Bay she would lose her insurance and the Capt's orders are not to go near it.

I have been singularly unfortunate as regards length of passage but I trust it is all ordered for the best by the Dispenser of all events, and my course is to rest in whatever he has determined.

I dreamed a curious dream about home last night and have thought a good deal about it since.

No divine service on board to day. I may say also no fear of God. Read over several chapters of the Bible &c.

5 p.m. Put about Ship. We had kept on as near shore as was safe and saw the breakers against the shore rising, I am sure, far above our main mast. Table mountain has a cloth upon it tonight and we expect a blow.

18 March 1839. Monday

Stood off shore again all last night but had the satisfaction of seeing the wind gradually veered round to South. This morning it is nearly calm, or nearly so, and we put about again with all sail set. The breeze freshened a little at midday and kept gradually turning round to west and it is now north west. Of course we took every advantage and at Sunset found ourselves in a direction to double the Cape. We have held on since, keeping a good look out for land, and we expect to be clear of the Cape of Good Hope tomorrow morning.

Since I have been writing, land was seen ahead and we have put about and are in circumstances more perilous than any in which we have yet been from a lee shore. The breeze too freshens and it is anything but comfortable at this hour of night. I shall not sleep much, I know, but will lie down a little to rest.

19 March 1839. Tuesday

Last evening proved favourable after all and, in again putting about this morning, we are in a position to get quite clear of the Cape. A home bound East Indiaman passed us deeply laden this morning and a smart little Brig is standing on before us.

We are scudding before a light breeze and passing headland after headland of this rugged coast. We shall, if fortunate, reach Algoa Bay tomorrow evening or Thursday morning and so shall get on by degrees. I have prepared one letter to send home to Scotland to my Uncle. I shall try to get a newspaper or two to send to other friends to intimate to them that I am well—I am well in health still and expect to have a little enjoyment on shore.

20 March 1839. Wednesday

We had a very boisterous night, squally with heavy rain and a heavy sea and to day it is much of the same character. We are coasting along shore and passing one abrupt and barren headland after another of this apparently barren country. Indeed we are standing rather too near shore, sailing as we are close to the wind.

This is apparently a most dangerous coast. But there are few rocks or reefs—and deep water clear under land.

21 March 1839. Thursday

Last night was remarkable for heavy thunder storms and with very vivid lightning. I saw the power of the electric fluid in a manner I never did before.

About 6 oClock in the evening I was standing on the quarter deck, when suddenly I saw a ball of fire descend and a loud report as of a cannon. It was however a thunder bolt, which fortunately struck one of the anchors which had acted as a conductor and burst. Several of the crew and passengers on the forecastle felt a concussion, and some of them imagined they saw fire, but I think the anchor must have dissolved the ball and so made it incapable of doing further damage. Every part of the Ship was examined but no injury had been done, altho instances have been known of a Ship being sunk in this way.

It poured all night and, there being little wind, all hands were kept on deck to wear the Ship off shore, as she was fast drifting in with the current. But the wind favoured us on two tacks and we got her off.

This morning we have a clear day and fine weather. About midday we got in sight of the last headland to be got round before putting into Algoa Bay. The wind however has failed us, and we shall not get near it to day. The coast looks better now and it rises to a considerable height.

Another and second instance of mortality occurred on board this morning, and one of a very melancholy nature. It is the wife of a man named Durieu, a 'jack of all trades' who with a large family are passengers on board. He had been bred to the law and had,

I suppose, married this woman when possessed of better prospects than he is now. She was evidently a woman who had seen better days, and who had possessed considerable personal attractions. Her mother*, an old woman who had accompanied her merely for the purpose of being near her daughter, has had the melancholy duty to close her eyes. She has left a large and helpless family—one child about 6 months old.

She was quite healthy and looked well when she came on board, and indeed she seemed to enjoy herself very much at Rio de Janeiro. But shortly after we sailed she became ill and, partly I think through grief of mind, and the absence of proper food, and other things necessary for her recovery, she gradually became worse, until this morning that she died amidst great suffering—thus showing us how uncertain human life is.

Her husband is a person of a depraved and unfeeling nature†, and does not seem much affected with his loss. He has expressed his desire that she

---

* The mother of Lucy Durieu was Mrs Mary Taylor.
† In 1978, Dalma Morgan and Harry Poole published *Voyage of a Lifetime*, about the descendants of two *Planter* passengers, Daniel Crosby and Emma Durieu, who married and had many children. As just one example of Henry Durieu's 'unfeeling nature', it is noted in this book that he had left his two-year-old daughter at Port Elizabeth with a wealthy English couple, who later returned with her to London.

may be buried on shore if practicable, which will be done if we, as we expect, get into harbour tomorrow. If not, her remains must find a watery grave.[*]

There is just another woman on board sick at present. I have mentioned her before — she is wife of a person who was a missionary at Madagascar[†] and her constitution must have been completely shattered by 11 years residence in that Island. She has been sick ever since we left England.

Mrs Nicholson is a good deal better and bids fair to add one to the number of our passengers before we reach Adelaide. Our long voyage must have been more than she ever calculated upon. Her husband mentioned to me to day that he had been thinking a good deal about cutting his voyage short and remaining at Algoa Bay.

22 March 1839. Friday

This morning we thought that our position must make us very near the bay of which we were in search, and on getting an observation we found it very near the longitude. Having a good breeze we stood in quite near shore and literally examined every creek and

---

[*] The family Bible records that Lucy Durieu was buried at sea on 22 March.

[†] We later learn that these are Mr and Mrs Canham.

were as frequently disappointed (this does not say much for our seamanship; no matter it is true). At last we saw a long point of land stretching out into the Sea and found that we must weather it, so we stood off and at last got in sight of a reef of rocks stretching seaward off the point. We got round however and found the bay running inland and 3 vessels lying at anchor.

We had to beat in and, just as the sun set, dropped anchor. The Surgeon of the settlement came on board to see if we needed any 'physic'—and gave us permission to go ashore.

23 March 1839. Saturday

Came ashore this morning in company with Mrs & Mr E. A dreadful surf breaks upon the shore and renders it impossible to land any boat except one built for the purpose—very high in the bows.

The number of houses here is not great and they are built without much under. The streets are merely a gravel pit. The houses are built without much attention to elegance. It contains a population of about 2500, consisting of English & Dutch. Outside the Town are two separate Fingo villages*, which

---

* The Fengu are a Bantu people, originally dubbed by the English as the 'Fingo'.

are occupied by people employed during the day by the white people in the town. Their huts are regular wigwams, formed exactly like a bee hive and with a small opening in one side. Inside, they have the floor covered with a mat in which they sleep—they are mostly in the open air during the day.

The native inhabitants of this part are the Hottentots; but as they are too lazy to work, they live at a distance from the settlement. Their huts are of a poorer description still. They themselves are small in stature and are very filthy; they live upon the spontaneous produce of this soil and seem to eat every thing indiscriminately. There are a few Caffres* too—they are again a superior race, tall and generally well formed.

5 April 1839. Friday

To day I resume my journal as I have resumed my voyage on board the 'Planter'. She sailed from Pt Elizabeth Algoa Bay on Wednesday morning, but have had light and contrary winds so that we have not made much progress yet. I shall commence where I left off and give a short history of what passed with me at Algoa Bay.

---

* An older spelling of Kaffirs, which is today an offensive name for black Africans.

As soon as we stepped ashore and were looking about the place a stranger accosted us and desired us to walk in and see his garden, which we had been admiring. We did so and the man was very friendly, showing us a good deal of kindness. We were rather inclined to stay on shore while the Ship lay in harbour, but we could not think of putting up at the Hotel (the only one, where the other Passengers would be) so we found private lodgings in the house of a Cabinet maker and they turned out very comfortable and respectable indeed. We lived in family with him and his wife and one daughter (a very pretty young woman by the bye) and had every comfort and luxury we needed at about one quarter the expense the other passengers were put to elsewhere. He had a very good horse, of which I had the use whenever I chose. Mr Nicholson Sr joined us in our lodgings—he could not associate with the other Cabin Passengers, so hateful has their conduct become.

Our Capt, as usual, was going to sail again in a day or two; but on the Ship being examined, she was declared unfit for sea and ordered to be repaired. The work was commenced and the masts taken down and overhauled; but as it blew several days so hard that no communication could be had with the shore, the work was a good deal retarded and she could not be got ready till Tuesday night, when we came on board and we sailed on Wednesday morning.

I never spent 10 days more pleasantly. Walked about all day, or rode over the hills and returned to spend the evening in rational intercourse with my friends at home. The face of the country appears barren; but still the soil is fertile and needs only the hand of man to make it one entire Garden. Flowers of the most beautiful colours grow wild. We visited places where the view was most romantic and indeed altogether I never spent a more pleasant week. Mrs Elphick was almost as much affected at bidding adieu to the place and our newly acquired friends as if she had been leaving her home.

The people on the borders of Caffreland are frequently plundered by the Savages; but they never come so far southward as Algoa Bay. There is a small fort here, garrisoned by the Hottentots with an English commander, to guard the place. There are no beasts of prey within 50 miles—some snakes are sometimes seen, but they never do much injury. Draught bullocks are plenty and cheap. Horses plenty, not very good, but also cheap. Sheep & goats very plenty and good. Beef and mutton 3d per lb.

The original settlers who had come out about 1820 have generally done well; but it seems as if the Spirit of enterprize forsakes Englishmen as soon as they leave home and, as soon as they find they can live in ease, they cease to push the resources of their genius further. Hence it is that every public improvement is so far behind in Algoa Bay—14 bullocks are required to draw a wagon which one horse would draw in England. The only improvement in the roads is effected by the Hottentots who, being convicted of some crime, are compelled to work for a certain time in chains on their roads.

6 April 1839. Saturday

Very light wind this morning and unfavourable. We have got now on board animals of about every species—6 horses, 1 Cow, Sheep, pigs, poultry, monkeys, tortoises, Cats, dogs &c &c. Indeed it is a complete menagerie—and we are in a mess ten times worse than ever.

We as usual expect a short passage now, but there is no appearance of it yet as we have scarcely yet lost sight of land.

7 April 1839. Sunday

Calm this morning. About 10 oClock a breeze sprang up with heavy rain and squalls. Another Sabbath finds me tossed upon the Sea. It reminds me of the Sabbaths I used to spend at Home, tho it bears no resemblance to them except in name.

It reminds me too of 2 sabbaths at Algoa Bay, which exceeded any I have spent for many months now. Indeed altogether Algoa Bay in my memory is one of those Oases, or fertile spots in the desert of this world, on which the mind loves to dwell with fond remembrances. I heard a sermon at an Independent Chapel by a Mr Price, a plain straight-forward Scotsman. I visited a school established for the instruction of the Natives. It was an interesting sight and showed the difficulties those have to encounter, who go forward to preach the gospel to the heathen whose language they do not know and whose understandings they cannot hope to enlighten without the aid of divine grace.

No acknowledgement of God on board to day.

8 April 1839. Monday

Light breezes and calms again to day—and every appearance of a prolonged voyage still. Cape Wine and brandy at 3/. per Gallon are pretty plenty on board now and pretty freely indulged in, to the serious disturbance of a part of our passengers and me among the others. Vice still very prevalent on board. Indeed it seems as if all sense of decency were lost sight of and the most glaring acts of crime had lost their enormity altogether.

9 April 1839. Tuesday

This day possesses the same character as the preceding ones—viz calm and unclouded, towards evening a slight breeze which would scarcely ruffle a millpond and we move on sluggishly. It seems now pretty evident that our passage will be in all 7 months, if not more—indeed it is a regular cruise round the world.

I believe I mentioned that during the last 10 years at Algoa Bay there have been no less than 50 vessels driven ashore. The wind blows in two directions only, viz north west and south east, and if once it begins to blow hard, no vessel can possibly ride it out as the whole weight of the Indian Ocean rushes in with dreadful force. During the time our Vessel laid there we had one hard gale. I was on shore but was very apprehensive of danger to the Ship as she had been moored with only one anchor and, altho the other was thrown out, yet of course it had no effect till the first had parted or begun to drag, which latter never happens. They always part, and then the Ship invariably is driven ashore stern foremost. Tho' her quarter boat was driven ashore, having been parted from her stern, yet she held on very well.

10 April 1839. Wednesday

Calm again this morning. Towards midday a slight breeze, which increased towards evening. It is however rather unfavourable and leads us out of our course a little.

It will be a busy time in Scotland now, committing the precious grain into the earth, and all will be life and animation at the return of Spring. All that I have seen, tho' I have visited several quarters of the globe, seems to be but a poor compensation for the loss of one single day of the happiness I have enjoyed at home. I have however gained in many respects, and while I have not by any act of mine lost that peace of mind which is always the attendant on virtue, tho' temptations of many kinds have assailed me, I cannot blame my fortune in making me a wanderer, seeing it was my own choice. And thanks be to God that I have not visited foreign countries in vain, but have had my education enlarged by what I never expected to meet with—viz the opportunity of seeing so much of the world.

11 April 1839. Thursday

Fair wind this morning. We crowded every inch of canvass upon the ship and have a fair run. We have just about 100 degrees to make of easting of course in the high latitude in which we now are—these degrees are smaller than near the Equator.

The climate we are now in—viz 36½° south latitude & 34° E Lon.—is very agreeably mild. Chilly morning and evening, but altogether of a very congenial temperature. In going further eastward we expect strong breezes and even gales of wind, but these are quite tolerable when they are carrying us on our Voyage.

Health still reigns among our people, which is a great blessing as if otherwise it would throw us in a dreadful mess where so many people are confined in so small compass.

12 April 1839. Friday

Steady fair breeze to day still and we make considerable progress. In the evening we had a shower of rain which was succeeded by a calm of about an hours duration until the clouds had again parted, when we were again favoured with the breeze.

We are in Lat: 39° 4' S, Lon: 39° 3' E. The weather has been delightful ever since we left Algoa Bay. The sea as smooth as a Lake while we have been gliding over it at the rate of 6 or 7 knots an hour.

How much I wish that I could but penetrate the veil of distance, and for one moment catch a glimpse of the dear faces of my friends. I trust they are all happy. I am sure they will think that I must be ere this landed in Australia—however this is not the case. But thank God I am in circumstances, if not of comfort, at least not of misery; and, God willing, shall not be long in reaching the end of my voyage now, when I shall write to them all.

I say circumstances *not of misery* because I am sure no person of any principles of virtue could call himself quite comfortable while his eyes and ears were annoyed every day by people who have long since rendered themselves insensible to the admonitions of conscience, or of others, who being newly led away from the path of virtue, are gratifying their depraved senses by revelling in the ignominy of Vice. But I think it always best to mention the grounds upon which I make my conclusions and I am sure I have grounds enough when I mention the fact that those who I think must have been virtuous when they commenced this voyage are now so far degraded as to think themselves honoured by appearing every day clad from head to foot from the purse of a person who has in doing so robbed his own wife, who for anything I know is living in penury at home. I refer to the case of our Capt and his paramours, the Misses McGowan. And his example has been followed by more than one of his subalterns.

13 April 1839. Saturday

Steady breeze again this morning and we go on running down our longitude. We are now fast approaching the Country of our adoption—whether for better or worse remains to be determined. I trust for better to some of us, but it has every chance to be for worse to many of us.

14 April 1839. Sunday

We have a good breeze this morning and we go on very well. At sunrise they descried a Vessel astern just appearing upon the horizon. During the forenoon she gradually neared us and it very soon became evident that she would pass us before night. Her colours showed her to belong to England and after a little signalizing the colours were taken down and she came up very fast. About 4 oClock she dropped under our quarter and on speaking her we found that she was the schooner 'Kelpie' from London to China, out since 30 January. Such a contrast between that and our passage makes ones heart sick. But to see her gain so much upon us, in spite of all the sail we could crowd on, was very vexatious. She was not more than 120 tons burden.

We have had to day a form of divine service, but as usual very disgusting on account of the manner in which it is gone about. I hope it will not be long now before I am again among people who reverence God and observe his holy day.

15 April 1839. Monday

Lon: 46° 54' E. This commences the 21st week of our voyage.

Fresh breeze this morning. It increased during the forenoon to a pretty strong gale—it is however very favourable and we go on very fast.

This weather seems to do the horses on board a good deal of injury as they are so knocked about and become so timorous. There is one very pretty little pony belonging to Mr Alexander—I suppose designed for his wife. I had taken a great fancy to it, which he observed and said that I might have it for 100 guineas. He seems to have some idea of making money at least, as he only paid £10 for it.

16 April 1839. Tuesday

It blows very hard this morning and the Sea is rising very high. About midday we had a very strong gale and had to shorten sail. In the evening we had a very heavy Sea and were put under close reefs.

17 April 1839. Wednesday

After a very rough night we have less wind to day and the Sea has fallen a little. We have made these two last days 8 degrees of Easting, which shortens our distance very fast.

A circumstance has happened to day on board which shows in a remarkable manner the 'ills that flesh is heir to'. Mr Canham, whose wife I have before mentioned has been ill during the whole voyage and who is yet in a very poor state of health partly from family distress and partly I am afraid from habits of intemperance*, has become unsettled in his mind. I hope it will only be temporary, but it is a sad thing to look upon the wretched state of himself & family at present; but much more so to look into what must be their fate in future. Mr C. had been at first a shoemaker but, having received a fair education, had got himself in some way connected with the mission to Madagascar, which was at last broken up and Mr C., along with several more, returned to England.

I presume he found himself unable to make any provisions for himself there and is now again trying a foreign land. He found at Algoa Bay two friends and fellow missionaries who had settled there in

---

* It is unclear from James Bell's punctuation whether it is Mr or Mrs Canham who is intemperate—one suspects this is a failing of the husband.

preference to going to England. They entertained him & his family well while there and his wife looked much better in health. Since then I thought him still in better spirits, but during the last few days he has had a slight bodily illness which, in conjunction with too free use of ardent spirits*, has produced a low state of mind and the seat of reason has evidently suffered a shock.

No greater misfortune could possibly befall any person than this and it shows how one ought to improve the time God has put into our hands.

18 April 1839. Thursday

It blows very hard to day with sudden squalls and rain, it is also very cold and uncomfortable. The Sea does not yet run very high but must in a short time if it continues to blow.

19 April 1839. Friday

Last evening was the most boisterous we have yet had. The rain poured in torrents and the wind blew with amazing violence at times. Also it blew in sudden gusts, threatening destruction to every sail we could hoist. The Sea ran very high and the motion of the

---

* A nineteenth-century euphemism for strong distilled alcohol.

Ship was quite intolerable while the hoarse voices of our Seamen, particularly the first Mate bawling and swearing amid the blast, was quite terrifying.

This morning it is again clear. The dense black curtain which enveloped us being withdrawn, our Ship again carries her sails. There is however still a strong breeze and heavy Sea. We are making a good deal of way these few days and are now in Lon: 60° E, Lat: 43° S. This is a very high Latitude but it was unavoidable, in order to obtain fair winds to get to the Eastward, to make a good deal of southing. It is pretty cold however now in this part of the world.

This morning we saw a Ship to leeward. She was hauled nearer the wind than we. We neared each other during the day and about 4 oClock we crossed her bows at about 2 miles distance. She then passed us about ½ mile to windward, but showed no disposition to speak us. We hoisted her our ensign & number; she answered with her Ensign, which proved her a 'Yankee' with her 'Stars & Stripes'. She was a very fine Ship and had every appearance of being a Whaler. She like the rest was soon out of sight and left us to plod our weary way alone.

It again begins to blow tonight and the Sea runs mountains high. Our course has been SE. It is now E.

20 April 1839. Saturday

Fine clear weather this morning and a fair breeze.
We are making a good run. The Sea has fallen again
and is now smooth again. We have made a very great
days work these last 24 hours and are now in 66° E
which is just halfway between Algoa Bay and our
destination. We have been out 17 days and if we are
only another 17 days from the end of our voyage the
space is now not very great.

And with God's blessing I think I shall make it
out in good health.

21 April 1839. Sunday

Lon: 71° 23' E, Lat: 41° S. Good breeze this morning
again and we go on very smoothly. We are making
now great progress towards the end of our Voyage.
A form of divine service to day on board.

I have before mentioned the name of Mr Nicholson
Sr*, at first as a dogfighter but afterwards in a more
amiable character. He lodged with us at Algoa Bay
and has kept up an intimacy with me since. He is
married and is no doubt a very sensible man. His
wife is near her lying in. His brother however is of

---

* Mr Nicholson senior is Arthur Bolt Nicholson.

quite a different character; he has been a common sailor and has contracted all their habits and vices.

By a Fathers death, or in some way, they have come into possession of money with which they had resolved to go to S. Australia and, keeping together, endeavour to make the most of their money. They had accordingly fitted themselves out jointly, and set out. Mr Nicholson Sr has been in the army, and is a complete gentleman. At Madeira the dogfight was their first difference but, as the younger one has been almost constantly intoxicated, he has disgusted his brother very much, and they have had a good many petty differences.

However of late the younger brother has been paying his addresses to a daughter of Durieu's, whom I have before mentioned as a very great blackguard. The daughter is a mere child, but no matter—it seems he intends to make a woman and a wife of her, and has sent a letter to his brother to say that he wishes to be altogether separated from him and to have a division of the joint property they have with them. Old Durieu of course urges him on, and has already cost him some money. His brother has the bills of lading and other documents, which the younger man wishes to get possession of.

Mr Nicholson Sr came to me to day and related these circumstances, asking me what I would advise him to do in these circumstances. I said it was a very delicate matter to treat with a brother but still, when no better could be, he must just at once come to some arrangement with him, and let him then take his own course. The partnership could easily be dissolved by mutual consent expressed in writing and then, as it was always best to prevent litigation, they should choose neutral persons as arbiters who could divide the joint property equally between the two. But, as nothing could be done until we landed, I advised him not to take any notice of his brothers letters till then. Or, if he did, inform him that an arrangement would be come to then as of course his brother could not take any means of compelling him on board and might possibly come to his proper senses before the end of the voyage. And if he needed the assistance of any Agents, I could recommend him to Flaxman & Rowlands whom I knew to be respectable.

I have forgot to mention the history of a few flowers with which I have interspersed the leaves of this book. They are not now pretty nor dare I pretend to give them a name, but their merit consists in them having been gathered by my own hands from the shores of Africa where they grow wild and with their beauty and fragrance (now both lost) perfume the air.

22 April 1839. Monday

This day commences with a thick fog and occasionally a slight shower of rain. It is rather calm in the
morning but towards midday a breeze, which became
pretty fresh in the evening when the fog began to
disappear.

This is about the time of holding the Lockerbie
hiring market*, when the lads and lassies from all the
surrounding country are to be found treating each
other to 'snaps' & 'sweeties' and such a portion of
the 'mountains dew' as is sufficient to put them both
in a good humour with themselves and all around
them. While the merry jest and laugh goes round,
there are such kind enquiries as the following—'Are
ye hired?' 'Yes, are ye?' 'Yes.' 'Where do ye gan?' 'Oh
lass, I gan so & so.' 'What wages do ye git?' &c &c.
While those whose days of gallantry are gone by, sit
and enjoy themselves over a 'drap nappy'† and talk
of former days.

But at last the time of going home has arrived,
and each lass 'linked' to her favourite beau takes to

---

* Lockerbie, the Scottish town later famous as the place where
the bombed PanAm Flight 103 crashed in 1988, in the mid
nineteenth century held a market in April each year where
servants were newly hired. Clearly, from the description here,
this also provided a venue for romance.
† *Nappy* is a Scottish word for ale; a *drap* is a drop.

the road and they reach home before sunrise next morning. But the selection is not always quietly made—perhaps two have fixed their regards on the same object and then a trial of physical strength ensues, after which the Victor carries the prize and conducts the buxom fair one to her home while the vanquished skulks off in search of humbler game.

While I am writing, I hear them shortening sail and the Capt foretelling wind.

23 April 1839. Tuesday

Fresh breeze to day and fair, we have an excellent run and our distance is very fast shortening. The weather is remarkably thick and hazy and at the same time very cold.

24 April 1839. Wednesday

Fair breeze again this morning and clear. We again get our observations this morning, and find ourselves in the Lon: 80° 42' E, & Lat: 40° 30' S.

This morning there died, after an illness of nearly 3 weeks, being the whole time she had been on board, a bay mare bought by Mr Alexander at Algoa Bay. Her complaint, I believe, was hunger and rough usage by the motion of the ship; and stupidity of her owner & groom, who did not treat her in a proper way. There are 4 more on board dying by inches of the same diseases. The food allowed them not being sufficient in quantity to keep them in health & strength and their treatment being a compound of ignorance and carelessness.

It is amazing to my feelings to see such a waste of horse's life. These animals I am very fond of.

25 April 1839. Thursday

Fair breeze this morning and clear weather. Towards evening squally with rain and the wind varied a few points to the Westward.

I have read a novel somewhere having for its title 'Who Milked My Cow'* and our Capt has been obliged to ask the same question, and this morning he accused a young man, a servant of Mr Alexander's†, of milking his cow and taking the milk to some of the young women. The young man retorted rather insolently and the Capt struck him. Mr Alexander has been making enquiries into the matter, and I think

---

* *Who Milked My Cow: or The Marine Ghost* was written by Captain Marryat and published in *Bentley's Miscellany* in 1837. Today Marryat is best remembered for his semi-autobiographical novel, *Mr Midshipman Easy*, and his children's novel, *The Children of the New Forest.*

† The young man employed by Alexander would seem to be Robert Harris, aged eighteen, of Ipswich, one of the free emigrants recorded as being sponsored by Alexander.

we shall have a little bit of a row about it when we get to Adelaide.

We have still very strange work going on, on board. I should like very much that, when we arrive at the end of our voyage, there should be a sort of review of what has occurred and I think in all probability there will be.

8 oClock p.m. Wind right aft and a fresh breeze.

Mr Canham has a good deal recovered his right senses, but is still moping & melancholy.

I have been busy reviewing my clothing, viz there is nothing worn of the voyage, but many a thing needs washing.

26 April 1839. Friday

Lon: 86° E, Lat: 40° S. Fresh breeze again this morning and right aft. We scud along beautifully towards our destined port. Weather squally with heavy rain in the evening.

Mr Nicholson called to day to shew me a letter from his brother and an answer he intended to send. The letter was written in an ignorant & disrespectful way, such as no person would think of writing to any gentleman, and contained anything but an expression of brotherly affection. Mr N's answer was written in a more becoming style and contained a respectful announcement that the papers demanded were put away and could not be easily got at till we reached Australia.

This was merely a putting off until it appears whether his brother comes round to his proper senses. On his explaining this to me, I told him that it was a good enough plan, to temporize until his brother had time to reflect.

9 oClock p.m. Strong breezes, shortened sails.

27 April 1839. Saturday

Strong breeze again to day and squally weather. Sea running very high. But no one making a great deal of sailing.

This is our Capts birthday and while I am writing they are preparing a supper, to which some of the Passengers are invited. It is in our part of the Ship and I am sure we shall have a precious row before it is over.

I am not invited and am very glad of it as it wd only have put me to the trouble of refusing, as I never shall join any of their cabals. Only 4 of the Cabin passengers are going to attend. It is supposed that we shall have the Misses McGowan there. If they are, it will lay the Capstone of their disgrace.

No observations got to day, owing more to stupidity than want of opportunity.

28 April 1839. Sunday

Lat: 40° S, Lon: 96° E. Light breeze this morning and fine weather. Squally in the evening. It is amazingly cold now—in the morning & evening enough to freeze water, and we have occasionally very heavy hail showers.

Last night about a dozen persons sat down to supper on the occasion of the Capts birthday. I was invited to sit down with them but declined. It was a decided failure, in spite of brandy punches and every thing. They cd never get into any thing like jovial humour—indeed many of them never opened their mouths at all and, as they make no hesitation to say to day, had attended out of a desire not to offend the Capt, but against their own wills.

Of course they cd not separate however without a quarrel, and one Gent, having rather pointedly alluded to the *red nose* of another—the prominent feature in that persons countenance being a very fiery nasal organ—it produced a good deal of dispute, which was taken up by the Capt. The altercation ran high and ended in the Capt throwing down the 'gauntlet' to the Gent of the 'flaming nose', who accepted the challenge. But the where and the when the dispute is to be ended, whether with 'sword', 'pistol', 'fist' or what weapons, or who are to be seconds &c &c, has not yet been fixed on between these 'doughty men of honour'. It was after midnight before all was quiet and to day little mention has been made of the matter.

No divine service to day. The Doctor said that *it was too cold.* I am in hopes that I have only another Sabbath to spend on board the 'Planter' and I shall not regret it. Indeed it seems as if the drama could not be kept up any longer as a 'comedy', but must change its character and become a 'tragedy'; so the sooner the curtain drops the better. Provisions are becoming dreadfully bad and scarce on board.

½ past 9. Fair evening—and I am off to bed. Deus mecum sit!*

29 April 1839. Monday

Very strong breeze this morning and cloudy. It is not very favourable but is gradually coming round, and will be SW.

Nothing of consequence goes on, but we are all anxious, and happy at the prospect we have of soon reaching our destination, God willing.

Lon: nearly 100° E. It is very cold now, indeed piercing cold to day, and this shows what I have before heard, viz—that the cold is more intense in the

---

* James probably means 'Deus mecum est' (God is with me); 'Deus mecum sit' means 'May God be with me'.

same latitude south than north of the Line. We have just 38° of Easting to make now and then comes a change of scene and our eras, in the lives of all of us.

30 April 1839. Tuesday

Strong gale this morning with heavy squalls and rain. The wind has veered round to our starboard quarter and we are dashing along 8 or 9 knots an hour. It is still amazingly cold to day tho we have made half a degree further north. Our course is E ½ N: Wind SW.

I feel very anxious now to be at the end of my voyage and, as the distance lessens, will feel greater anxiety. It is now 156 days that I have been upon the Sea, and appears a long time indeed. During that time I have lived in the company of people whom I never would have desired to have become acquainted with and, tho' their manners have in no way affected mine, yet I cannot think of them without disgust, and fear that, as 'water wears away the flinty rock', so the coming in so much contact with them shd gradually undermine my own principles of virtue, and make me, as they have frequently attempted to do, no better than themselves. But thanks be to God who has kept me hitherto, & I trust that before long I shall have before my eyes a better example and again know what it is to live among people who know the aim for which they were made, and have respect to their latter end.

If parents knew what temptations their children have to meet with in the world, how anxious wd they be (like my dear Father was) to instil into their minds principles of good, and to watch over their growth until they strengthen. And then how wd vice decrease, and ruin be averted by many a promising child. It is only after a person has been for some time mixed with the world that he can see its vices and its follies, and he is fortunate who sees them time enough to save himself from the danger of falling prey to its allurements. Vice too assumes so many shapes that, to any but careful observers, she would seem endowed with all the charms of virtue.

1 May 1839. Wednesday

Fresh breeze again this morning, but cloudy and with rain. It is also remarkably cold. A great many birds flying about the Ship, viz Albatrosses and *penguins.* Indeed we have never been a day without seeing birds since we left the Cape of Good Hope.

This day commences in Scotland one of the finest months of the year. And is always distinguished by the name of the 'pleasant month of May'. It has such a mixture of spring and summer in it as to make it particularly agreeable. But on the other hand it is only the commencement of winter & the rainy season at Adelaide.

2 May 1839. Thursday

Lon: 108° E, Lat: 41° S. Strong breeze again this morning and fine weather—running 8 to 10 knots. We expect to reach our destination in 8 or 10 days now. But they seem to me as long as many years.

People all well on board still—indeed very well considering the crowded state of the Ship & the mode of living &c. It seems that the proportion of deaths is very much less than among the same number of people during the same time on land. Scurvy in a few instances is now appearing, but very rare and those who are affected with it will soon recover on their getting again on land.

How thankful ought we to be to the Giver of every good gift for his goodness to us all. But on the contrary there is nothing but discontentment, and I am sure a good many of them will be very sorry when they have to leave the Ship as they are living perhaps better than they have ever done before.

3 May 1839. Friday

Lon: 112° E, Lat: 40° S. Strong breeze again this morning and fine weather. It is cold still, but it is cheering now to be sweeping along day after day before a good wind.

> *The waves behind impel the waves before,*
> *Wide rolling, foaming high, & tumbling to the shore*[*]

The prospect of reaching the end of our voyage occupies the mind with pleasing thoughts, tho' at the same time with anxious faces.

4 May 1839. Saturday

Strong breeze again to day and we sail on very well. Expect the end of our Voyage before this day week.

5 May 1839. Sunday

Breeze all night very strong—motion of the Ship very unpleasant. Sea running very high.

This morning I heard the news of our having last night received an addition to our numbers by Mrs Nicholson's giving birth to a daughter.[†] Poor child—the storm of last night, which with its howling

---

[*] This couplet is from Alexander Pope's famous translation of Homer's *Iliad*, Book XIII.

[†] This was Ann Jane Nicholson, who was subsequently baptised in Trinity Church, Adelaide, on 17 June 1839, with her date of birth recorded in the register as 5 May.

blasts ushered thee into existence upon the bosom of the mighty waters, was only an anthem of the ocean of life, stormy and tempestuous, which thou hast yet to cross.

Mother and child doing well.

6 May 1839. Monday

Last night was particularly stormy and unpleasant. The wind wheeled round every point of the compass and at last fixed in the south west. About 6 this morning it became very hazy and rain fell in torrents accompanied by such a gale of wind as I trust I shall never again experience at Sea.

The Capt, who had kept the middle watch, had just turned in and the 2d mate was on watch. The gale came down with such fury that it burst the main tack in one instant, and away went the sail to pieces with the wind. The mate, who had been so stupid as not to perceive its coming on, called all hands to secure the flapping sail. But while they were attempting this, away went the fore yard in 2 halves and left all the canvass to chafe about the mast. The jib was reduced to rags, and all that was left was the double reefed main topsail.

The gale continued with tremendous fury till about 9 oClock, when it cleared up and moderated a little. But while it lasted, I cannot describe any thing like its fury. The masts, after the sails had been all rent, quivered and shook in the wind. The sea came on in billows almost as high as our masts, and we were at one time suspended on the summit of a huge wave, at another plunged down headlong into the gulph between and, as we had no sails to keep her steady, she was at times almost lying on her side, and the water on the both sides spouting over her decks.

The Capts cow was thrown over the long boat upon the deck, and is in a deplorable state, as are all the horses and live stock. As soon as it moderated, we brought her to under her stay & main trysail, and got the wreck cut away; but we are in a very disabled state and I trust to God to send us fine weather until we get her again into some repair.

The Sea is very high still and she rolls very heavily, but as it is now tolerably calm and settled looking I trust it will be a fair night. Fortunately we were a long way from a lee shore, else we had been cast away without a chance of escape.

It is very cold.

7 May 1839. Tuesday

This morning is very fine indeed with a pretty fresh steady breeze and, tho' we cannot aid our progress much by setting sails, still we move on a little. Carpenter and 2 or 3 volunteers employed at the making of a new fore yard, which I trust they will finish tomorrow. Got the main sail & jib repaired and rebent to day and we only want our fore yard up to put us in a tolerable state for finishing our Voyage. We are to day in Lat: 40° S, Lon: 125° E and are now coming to close quarters with the land, having only 14 more degrees to make altogether.

The scenes of our Drama become daily more intricate and indeed I can scarcely now see where it is to end. The Capt and Surgeon having last evening disagreed and begun to review each others conduct, the dispute ran so high as to provoke the former to knock the latter down with his fist. And I presume will be made pay for this liberty, which will open up a long account to be settled by both parties.

8 May 1839. Wednesday

Lon: 128° E, Lat: 40° S. This day is very fine with a light breeze and clear weather. All hands busy with the fore yard, which was got up in the afternoon. The sail will be bent upon it tomorrow morning, so we shall have the pleasure of again seeing her under the whole of her Canvass.

This day commences my 23d year. On reflecting on the past period of my life, I feel many affecting sensations; on looking forward, the future seems dark and obscure, but is perhaps wisely hid from my sight.

I however put my trust in that God who has never yet forsaken me, and who I trust will make me pass all the birthdays appointed to me at least as happily as I have done this.

My fellow passengers all congratulated me this morning on the occasion. If we are fortunate, a very few days must now bring us to the end of our Voyage—and then will commence a new scene. The hurry & bustle of business will again occupy me and I shall have less time to spend as I please, and this journal must of course cease.

9 May 1839. Thursday

Cloudy this morning with a light breeze. Towards midday breeze increased and in the evening blew pretty fresh. We have got our foresail bent to day and are again under the whole of our Sails. It gives me a good deal of pleasure to see our Ship again fully rigged after the dismantled appearance she had.

We are begun to look out for land and it is amusing to hear one after another of our passengers calling out that he sees land, while it still proves to be only a Cape-fly-away.* We are in Lon: 130° E to day and, having only 8 more degrees to make, we imagine

---

* *Cape fly-aways* (the usual spelling) were low cloud banks that could be mistaken for landforms on the horizon.

what we so much wish. Indeed the appearance of the clouds is frequently such as very often to favour the delusion.

I have to day been reading a little work containing an address by a Christian Pastor to his people in which he quotes the following. Speaking of sinners:

And to their everlasting anguish still,
The thunder from above responding spoke
These words, which, through the caverns of perdition
Forlornly echoing, fell on every ear:
'Ye knew your duty, but ye did it not.'
And back again recoiled a deeper groan.
A deeper groan! Oh, what a groan is that![*]

Hear this ye apostates from the ways of Virtue and tremble. May God always preserve me in the paths of righteousness, which are smooth paths and which lead to happiness & peace, is my earnest wish and prayer.—J.B.

---

[*] This is an extract from Book 1 of *The Course of Time, A Poem in Ten Books* by the Scottish poet Robert Pollok and published in the last year of his life, 1827. It was an instant bestseller in its day.

10 May 1839. Friday

The breeze increased during last night and this morning it blows a pretty strong gale. We are put under close reefs and move on but slowly as the wind is rather unfavourable and we are close hauled. We have now a change of the appearance of the Sea, and the sky too is of a different appearance—changed from the steady and fixed appearance it has out to sea. At times it is mild and the air soft; at others chilly and stern. But altogether such as to indicate land to be at no great distance.

11 May 1839. Saturday

A most Charming morning. Air sharp and bracing. Very light breeze, and we make but little way. Evening clear and beautiful—the heavens studded with innumerable stars, which are those which shine alike upon the lands of my fathers and that of my adoption. We feel rather anxious at night now and keep a good look out.

12 May 1839. Sunday

We have made very little progress these 24 last hours and, altho' we have looked most anxiously all day, no certain glimpse of the promised land has been obtained. We have been deceived by many false appearances—not a cloud has darkened the sky but has presented to our imaginations land in some shape or other, and the universal cry is *land land*. Our reckoning, if at all to be depended on, makes it at no great distance.

This day is very fine and is I hope a fair specimen of Australian weather. This is the 24 Sunday since we left England and I think quite a long enough time to have been on one Voyage. No prayers on board to day—Sailors busy bending chains upon the anchors &c.

13 May 1839. Monday

This morning displayed to our eager eyes what we have so long looked and wished for, viz *land* and Australian land too. But the question was what part of the land *is it*—is it Kangaroo Island or the Mainland or what. Well these questions are not so easily answered.

But at last we, according to the best of our nautical skill, conclude that we have got too far north and put about. Bearing up SE appearances towards evening rather justify this conclusion, so we hold on.

It has been very calm all day. A dead calm at midday and we have been drifting a little towards land, but we have got a breeze in the evening.

The appearance of this part of the coast is very barren, but it is only a strip along the shore so cannot be considered a fair specimen. It is not very safe sailing so near a coast so little known, but I hope our Capt will be cautious and keep off.

14 May 1839. Tuesday

Last evening about Sunset a strong breeze sprang up and we stood south E & E. We only wanted to make round, or point a few miles off. But very stupidly the ship was allowed to run on till 4 this morning, when we have too little daylight.

When the sun rose we cd see no vestige of land and cd not conceive where we had got to. On getting our observations we found, or rather suspected, that we were southward of Kangaroo Island and steered SE. At Sunset we saw a long stretch of low land to windward and a squall coming on. The wind shifted and we steered directly SW—the direction in which the land was seen.

It blew pretty fresh and she roared thro it until we became very much afraid as we had no certainty of where we were and knew land to be at no great distance. The Capt however persisted in carrying on. Indeed he had become selfwilled on account of remarks made by the Passengers on his seamanship.

At 10 at night however we saw land, tho' it was very dark, and hove to till next morning.

The fact is, as he thinks to day and tells me, tho he says he wishes it to be concealed from the other passengers, the land we first made was Kangaroo Island and he made the mistake of steering S instead of N, thinking it to have been the Mainland. If so, we go in search of the Backstairs passage.*

15 May 1839. Wednesday

This morning we were close in land, but what land nobody could tell. It was in the form of a bay and very smooth water. We had put round Southward but, on examining the Chart, we found a place very like it in Kangaroo Island westward of the Backstairs passage, which is a narrow passage between the Island of Kangaroo and the Mainland. Merely on this supposition, we put again about and fortunately our surmises were right and we have again *found*

---

* The so-called Backstairs Passage is the narrow entrance to St Vincent's Gulf from the east; it lies between Kangaroo Island and Cape Jervis on the mainland. Captain Beazley, with his characteristically stubborn incompetence, had totally overshot the Gulf, which is Adelaide's harbour. He would have intended to enter the Gulf from the west, via Investigator Strait, which lies to the north of Kangaroo Island, rather than the Backstairs Passage, which lies to its east.

ourselves, after having made the circuit of Kangaroo Island, which has been any thing but a pleasant one.

We had a beautiful day to day and got thro the passage into the gulph of St Vincent and are tonight lying hove to, intending to put into harbour tomorrow. I need not say that we have most delightful anticipations of at last ending a long and tedious voyage, which has been any thing but agreeable.

Tho we have come up Backstairs passage, still we are now near the end of our voyage and must just excuse every deficiency of skill in our Capt and other annoyances. As pleasure is sweet after pain, so the pleasure of having gone thro so much will be pleasant in the reflection.

I have only seen the *coast* which is pretty and, tho not rising into high peaks, is very varied and beautiful. Tomorrow I hope to step ashore at Adelaide and introduce myself to Messrs Flaxman & Rowlands.

So ends James Bell's account of his 'long and tedious voyage', but on the flyleaf of his journal are written four further lines, presumably noted at a later time:

Stirling Stable
25/. a week move on a weeks notice—
Entry 2 Septr 1839
Monday Sept 26 commenced lodging in Town—

237

May 1835 —

I need not say that we have
most delightful anticipations of
at last ending a long and tedious
voyage which has been any
thing but agreable and tho
we have come up Backstairs
passage still we are now near
the end of our voyage and must
just excuse every deficiency
of skill in our Capt. and
other annoyances and as pleasure
is sweet after pain so the
pleasure of having gone thro'
so much will be pleasant in
its reflection — I have only
seen the coast which is pretty
and tho' not rising into
high peaks is very varied and
beautiful —

        Tomorrow I hope to
step ashore at Adelaide and
introduce myself to Messrs
Flaxman & Rowland —

Stirling Stable

25/ a week more on a weeks
notice —

Entry 2 Septr 1835

Monday Septr 26 commenced
lodging in Town —

_____

26

EPILOGUE
BY ANTHONY LAUBE

When James Bell and the rest of the weary travellers on
board the *Planter* finally found their way into the Port
River, their first view of South Australia was a collection of
slab huts and rough wharves among sandhills and swamp.
The port was not much less advanced than Adelaide itself,
eight kilometres away. And even here the chaotic nature of
the journey was not quite over, as Captain Beazley delayed
the unloading of his passengers, earning himself a fee for
keeping waiting the bullock carts sent by the emigration
agent to transport the travellers to the city.[1]

A few weeks earlier, a new arrival had described Adelaide
as something resembling a gypsy camp:

---

1 Letter of complaint to Governor Gawler from Thomas Beazley, 30
   May 1839 (GRG 35/5/no. 20).

It was in fact an extensive woodland, with here a solitary tent and there clusters of erratic habitations. There were canvas tents, tarpaulin tents, wurleys made of branches, log huts, packing-case villas, and a few veritable wooden cottages . . .[2]

The only substantial buildings were the brick homes of three of the wealthier settlers, the large offices of the South Australian Company, and two taverns, already open for business (even in what was later to be dubbed 'the city of churches' the places of worship were rougher and fewer than the pubs). In these surroundings a population of over 4000 had gathered. Stories were told of how these first residents were sometimes lost at night within the forest of trees and thick wattle scrub which was the square mile laid out for the city. By May 1839, many of the massive trees had been removed from the newly marked streets, leaving great holes which the unsuspecting fell into—holes often filled with water from the early rains.

But even worse than the rough buildings and the difficulty in finding 'streets', the *Planter* travellers discovered as much turmoil now they were at last on land as they had experienced at sea. A month before the *Planter* set sail from London, Lieutenant-Colonel George Gawler, South Australia's second governor, and his family had arrived in Adelaide, sent in response to the unbridgeable disagreements which had

---

2 'Letters of a Septuagenarian: Adelaide in 1839', *South Australian Register*, 15 April 1878, p. 5.

divided the founders. The running of the colony had initially been based on a division of power between the first governor, Captain John Hindmarsh, and the Resident Commissioner (representing the Colonization Commissioners), James Hurtle Fisher. Fisher was a lawyer, and had mostly written his own job description, giving himself far wider powers than the governor wielded. The resulting clash of roles and personalities began on the voyage out, on board the *Buffalo*. On land, the senior officials—including the governor's private secretary, also the editor of the colony's first newspaper— either took sides or began their own factions.

While these power battles were being played out, the colony faced an acute shortage of labourers, including a shortage of surveyors. William Light, a friend of Hindmarsh, was Surveyor-General at the time. He had not been given enough staff or funds by the Colonization Commissioners to carry out his role, and his deputy, George Kingston, was sent back to England for reinforcements. The Commissioners sent Kingston back with a recommended alternate surveying method. Light promptly quit, followed by all his staff. At this point the Colonization Commissioners and the British Colonial Office stepped in; they recalled Hindmarsh, fired Fisher, and appointed Lieutenant-Colonel Gawler as 'a godly man' to fill the roles of both Governor and Resident Commissioner. On his arrival in Adelaide in October 1838, Gawler voluntarily added to his workload the roles of assistant surveyor and explorer, while his wife distributed religious tracts and established Bible classes.

Gawler arrived to a settlement living mostly in tents, waiting for their land purchases to be surveyed. The over-worked public servants, and indeed many settlers, were on the brink of starvation. All this Fisher had hidden from the Commissioners, whose secretary, Rowland Hill, wrote to Gawler, 'Every fresh dispatch from the Colony renders the Commissioners more and more anxious . . .'[3] A man of action, Gawler took over the surveying himself, until he lured the explorer Charles Sturt as Surveyor-General. When a fresh party of surveyors arrived from England unannounced, courtesy of the Commissioners, Gawler wisely amalgamated them with members of Light's team who had returned to work for him.

In the meantime, a growing stream of immigrants under free passage poured into South Australia. This much-needed labour supply brought its own problems, particularly housing and food shortages. Added to this was an influx of 'bad characters', including runaway sailors and ex-convicts from the other colonies. Gawler established a police force, and toyed with the idea of an Aboriginal unit. From London, Rowland Hill pestered Gawler for reports:

Referring you to my letters to Mr Fisher of the 31st January 1838, and my despatch to yourself of the same year no. 24, requiring a report on the conduct of the

---

3 Copies of letters to the officers of the Colonization Commissioners for South Australia, 1836–1840 (GRG 48/5 24 July 1838).

emigrants selected by the agents, I have to call your attention to the fact that such reports are now due . . . and that according to the agreement with the agents, the whole agency for the emigrants by these ships must now be paid whether such emigrants have been well or ill-selected, a result which, in all probability will not only subject the colony to unnecessary charge; but will have the mischievous effect of rendering the agents careless in the performance of their duties, and thus deteriorate the quality of the emigrants selected hereafter.[4]

The Commissioners were finding that Wakefield's ideal system could not depend on idealistic support from the innumerable individuals needed to put the show on the road. Families well able to pay for their passage were obtaining free tickets, while others were leaving without fulfilling their obligation of paying for their children. One John Rhodes travelled out with a lady who was not his wife, leaving his legal spouse to complain to the Commissioners—who promptly sent her out after him.[5] The Commissioners were greatly concerned by letters from the settlers describing a shortage of basic foodstuffs, forcing them to allocate £3000 for the purchase of flour from merchants trading with the other Australian colonies.[6] Everything was slowed down by

---

4 Ibid., p. 326.

5 Ibid., p. 349.

6 Ibid., pp. 355–6.

the fact that each piece of correspondence, like the travellers themselves, took six months or even longer to travel between Adelaide and London. Sometimes there came no reply at all.

Then, at the beginning of May 1839, just two weeks before the arrival of the *Planter*, while Gawler was away looking for arable land with Sturt, two shepherds were speared to death by Aborigines. Until then, reasonably amicable relations had existed between the indigenous people and the settlers, even though the founding of Adelaide had cost the local Kaurna people dearly. Their prized hunting ground had become the site of the capital, where Europeans now crashed around laying out streets, removing trees and shooting off guns—in the process frightening away kangaroos, emus and other food sources, which they often took for themselves. (Additionally, the Europeans collected kangaroo skins as a substitute for their usual sources of leather.) In a very short time the traditional people had been reduced to begging for rations, yet there had not been any serious clashes until the spearings.

When the *Planter* travellers arrived in Adelaide, they found the residents in a state of frenzy whipped up at public meetings. Adding to the hysteria, the *Register* newspaper had misreported that the Aborigines had killed four people, rather than the actual two.

But despite the inadequate living arrangements, the held-up surveys and this latest trouble, not everything was disaster and muddle in the young settlement. The settlers—most of them young—must have found some cause for optimism in the fine sunny days of an Adelaide autumn. The canvas capital was surrounded by a broad expanse of ancient eucalypts within fine grasslands, giving the impression of an English park. James Bell's fellow passenger, the teenage Scottish weaver Alexander Hay, would later describe riding in a cart through the 'scrub' during those first weeks, and coming across (in what would one day be the suburb of Hindmarsh) the 'Land of Promise' Hotel. For young Hay the name seemed a hopeful sign of all that lay ahead of him in his new life.[7]

So what were the ultimate fortunes of the *Planter* travellers, the many named and unnamed characters of James Bell's journal? What became of the unlikely group that had been thrown together for more than six months on the high seas?

The travellers certainly did not waste time in getting on with their lives in their new home. Almost as soon as they were ashore, there was a flurry of marriages at Trinity Anglican Church. In August 1839, just five months after his wife's death at sea, Henry Durieu was married in the crude wooden first Anglican Church to a woman employed to look after his younger children—somewhat to his family's horror.[8] One month later, Captain Holmes, one of the rowdy cabin passengers, married Ann Merrett, a servant girl he

---

7 *South Australian Chronicle*, 15 April 1882, p. 21.

8 Dalma Morgan, *Voyage of a Lifetime*, Brighton SA, 1978, p. 59.

had brought out on the *Planter*. (And another nine months later, a baby girl was born.)

Caroline Strong, a farm servant from Wiltshire, married James Stabbington; and two more servant girls—Durieu's niece, Honora Keane, and Hannah Blackeby—married James Foster and James Winfield respectively. In June 1840, Daniel Crosby, a miner from Lincolnshire, married the eldest Durieu daughter, Emma, whom he clearly met on board ship, while in December Leamon Doe, the cabinetmaker from Suffolk, married Louisa Hughes. The following year, Joseph Nias, another rowdy, married Mary Odgers.

The death of an Elizabeth Taylor is recorded on 10 December 1839. Presumably this is the tipsy woman Bell refers to as breaking her leg during the voyage. At the time of her death she was still living in the temporary arrivals' accommodation at 'Emigration Square'.

The later lives of some of the *Planter* travellers are well documented. Alexander Hay, the pious young Scot (who was never mentioned in James Bell's journal), opened a shop in Rundle Street and grew to be one of the city's richest men, with landholdings all over Adelaide and a seaside 'castle' at Victor Harbor. Thomas Mugg, also not mentioned in the journal, did not thrive like Hay. A London carpenter, he changed careers to become the first schoolmaster in the Adelaide suburb of Mitcham, where a hill bears his unlikely name. Robert Fiveash's name was perpetuated in finer form through his clever daughter Rosa, the botanical artist.

Hannah Blackeby's nephew, meanwhile, was the founder of a chain of sweetshops.

Others appear in and out of the Adelaide newspapers for almost a century. Charles Canham, youngest son of the disappointed Madagascar missionary, would for decades keep the *Planter* name in the press, attending the colony's foundation commemoration ceremony at the Old Gum Tree, Glenelg, until the late 1920s, when he was almost 90. Daniel Higgins had a long and varied working life between being overseer of the printing department of the *Register* newspaper and a west coast farmer. Even one of the mutinying crew would resurface years later, as a respected long-time employee of the South Australian postal service. The obituary of third mate William Witherick glosses over the fact that he almost certainly jumped ship in Adelaide, by simply saying he 'decided to remain'.[9]

But many of the *Planter* travellers disappear into obscurity, perhaps soon moving on to the older, more established colonies such as Tasmania or New South Wales—despite the Colonization Commissioners' best attempts to make it worthwhile for their 'ideal emigrants' to stay in South Australia. Even those known to have stayed are elusive in scanty old records. Of the handful with whom James Bell formed friendships during the long voyage, Alexander McLean eventually established a farm at Gawler Hills, north

---

9 *Advertiser*, 30 August 1897, p. 3.

of Adelaide. Here a daughter was added to the three sons he and his wife brought to South Australia.

William Elphick, the chemist—Bell's fellow intermediate passenger—briefly opened a business in Adelaide. He then became government assayer for the huge Burra Burra copper mine, which effectively saved South Australia from bankruptcy in 1845. William and his wife Susanna had a large family born to them in South Australia. Their youngest son, Edward, became a well-known doctor. William Elphick collapsed and died suddenly at the Adelaide Railway Station in 1869, but Susanna lived to be 87, dying in 1899. Bell would no doubt have approved of the Elphicks' long involvement in Christian works and societies.

The disputing brothers, Arthur and Robert Nicholson, did work together, at least initially. In 1840 they had a small but thriving property of eleven acres named Zetland Farm close to the city. The 1841 Census showed that Arthur and his wife Margaret had nicknamed their little daughter born at sea 'Oceana'. By 1846 Arthur had given up farming to become an assistant police inspector. In 1850 he was a mere constable; then, like his brother, he disappears altogether.

Samuel and Rebecca Alexander, with their baby and quantity of servants, settled at genteel Walkerville, a fledgling Adelaide suburb. Apart from the birth in 1840 of a son, John Edward, they too disappear. The Alexanders were members of a wealthy Quaker family of bankers from Ipswich, and possibly returned to England.

John Canham, the disappointed Madagascar missionary with the sick wife, settled at Hackham, south of Adelaide. Canham died in 1881, aged 84. His wife Mary Anne lived a further fifty years after arriving on the *Planter*, dying in 1889. A son, John junior, was run down and killed by an Adelaide horse tram two years later, in 1891.

And what of the notorious minister/teacher/brewer/ assistant ship's surgeon James Macgowan and his nine daughters? The details of Macgowan's career are peppered through old newspaper reports and advertisements, both in England and Australia. Macgowan, as James Bell observed at sea, seemingly used any means he could to advance his prospects. As soon as he was in Adelaide, advertisements appeared in the newspapers:

> Education. Mr Macgowan, who brings with him from Liverpool the highest testimonials of moral character and of success in teaching, intends in two or three weeks to open a classical and commercial school-room . . .[10]

James Bell no doubt read the notice with disgust.

One month later, a further advertisement announced the imminent opening of the said school in Coromandel Place, with a complementary school for young ladies to be run by Mrs Macgowan and her daughters, and an evening class for workers. Macgowan also advertised his 'famous'

---

10 *South Australian Register*, 1 June 1839, p. 6.

school textbooks, whose sales he claimed had run into 20,000 copies in England.[11]

The following year, Macgowan received some unwanted publicity. Writing in August 1839 to a teacher friend in Liverpool, he had described his first weeks in South Australia (giving an insight into the Macgowans' ongoing relations with Captain Beazley) before lambasting the colony:

Five months elapsed from the period of our leaving the Downs, till we arrived at this place. We anchored in 'the Creek' on the 16th May, but the difficulties and delays we met with were such, that it was not until the 22nd July that I could open school. I have seven boys; I am going to open an evening school, and my wife a girls' school to-morrow. This is the *first* letter that I have sent from this colony.

The Captain was very kind to us during the passage, and also on coming to anchor. Finding provisions so high, he pressed us to become his guests in the cabin, for three weeks, hoping in that time our house would be ready for us . . .

Most of the people are very much disappointed in this place; many who came out as cabin passengers have been very much at a loss what to do to exist; some have become carters (on their own account); some that have a talent for

---

11 Ibid., 6 July 1839, p. 3.

it have undertaken jobs as carpenters, painters &c. Several have laid out their few hundred pounds in building pise cottages to let. So many ships are still arriving with hundreds of passengers, that both rent and provisions are extremely high. This colony has not produced grain sufficient for *one day's consumption*. In fact there is next to a famine both here and in Van Diemen's Land; which we have been draining, as well as Sydney . . .

Now, at the best season for it, there is scarcely any grass within six or seven miles of Adelaide. I believe there is none in the colony with the blades close together . . . The town has the appearance of a race-ground, with booths and huts for temporary accommodation in all directions, and here and there a brick or stone house, and in one place a considerable village.[12]

Macgowan would later claim he had not expected the letter to be published—if he had, he could not have realised that it would appear in print all over Britain. First the Liverpool *Mercury* published the letter, from where it was copied by other newspapers. Finally it appeared in the famous, and widely read, *Chambers' Edinburgh Journal*. James Macgowan could never have dreamed that nine months after he wrote the letter it would appear in print in Adelaide, amid a torrent of indignation in the *Register*:

12 *Chambers' Edinburgh Journal*, 18 April 1840, p. 101.

More inconsiderate, rash, and incorrect statements were never penned. We are indeed scarcely less amazed at the wild and reckless assertions of this individual, than that no prompt effort has been made by him to explain or modify what it is possible he may have reported on the false information of others.[13]

Macgowan rushed to write to the *Register*, admitting he was wrong on some counts, but not all. This did not stop the newspaper from enlarging on how 'grossly incorrect' the statements in the letter had been. 'We have only one word of advice to give to Mr Macgowan and to all new comers—never to give an opinion regarding anything they have not actually seen themselves.'[14]

After this blow, Macgowan launched a media campaign with front-page advertisements for the school, describing his teaching methods and quoting accolades for his teaching manuals. The school was now in Stephens Place, near North Terrace, and Macgowan spent the following years writing letters and giving lectures about his methods, and criticising the proposed 1850 Education Bill. His school was successful in a small way. Education returns for 1851 (by which time the Macgowans were receiving government assistance for the school) show there were 28 students in

---

13 *South Australian Register,* 29 August 1840, p. 2.
14 Ibid., 5 September 1840, p. 2 and 12 September 1840, p. 3.

the boys school, and 20 in the girls.[15] James Macgowan died in April 1856. Mrs Macgowan continued the school until 1859; she died in 1860, in Tasmania, at the home of her second daughter, Agnes.

The infamous Macgowan daughters initially helped in the school. Agnes married Dr Thomas Smart in Tasmania in 1844. What she was doing in Tasmania is a mystery. Helen Macgowan married widower Edward Collingwood in 1851; and soon after their father died, Jessie and Mary Macgowan were also both married—to Samuel Sprigg and George Wollaston respectively. Mary and George Wollaston had six children. The eldest of the lively Macgowan girls, Susannah, died single in 1869, as did fourth daughter Elizabeth. Jean, one of the youngest, lived on in Adelaide until 1904.

Samuel Harris, the ship's doctor, made a reappearance in South Australia in 1851. '[H]aving from ill health been obliged to leave England,' he reminded the good people of Adelaide that he was once surgeon superintendent aboard the *Planter*.[16] His practice was then in Franklin Street. One wonders if he ran into any of his former patients, including the Macgowans. But again, he seems to have disappeared after a short time.

And lastly, what of our man James Bell, the writer of the *Planter* journal?

---

15 Ibid., 9 August 1851, p. 3.
16 Ibid., 10 February 1851, p. 2.

The final entries in James Bell's journal are two short notes: he appears to have hired a horse from the Stirling Stable, and, 'Monday Sept 26 commenced lodging in town'. James had a prearranged position with a subsidiary of the South Australian Company, Flaxman and Rowlands. Charles Flaxman was George Angas's secretary, and had been sent to South Australia in 1838 to assist the group of German religious refugees Angas had sponsored. Once the group were settled, Flaxman began speculating using Angas's money. In partnership with Edward Rowlands he built the huge store mentioned in 1839 descriptions of Adelaide, and also bought the land later settled by Angas's Germans, the famous Barossa Valley. By the time James Bell arrived to take up his job in the Rundle Street store, Flaxman had been summoned by Angas to return to London to answer for his speculations with his master's money. Presumably James worked in the store in Rundle Street until almost the end of 1840. He clearly also lived in rooms at the store.

Only two more facts are known about the devout young Scotsman with the penchant for poetry—and for a certain lady back in Cumbria by the name of Perry. Predictably, following all his thoughts about God in his journal, his name appears in the records of the South Australian Presbyterians. The pastor, Ralph Drummond, brought a faithful and sizeable number of pious Scots together each Sabbath in the building that housed his weekday school in Angas Street. In early 1840, plans were made to build a church in Gouger Street, and on 6 October James was elected one of the 'managers' of the church. His name appears four times in motions at the election meeting.[17] The same month had seen the opening of the 'new port', and the 'Mr Bell' named in the long list of those present at the ceremony (a list which includes the Alexanders and Nicholsons) is possibly James.

The final known fact about James is a short notice printed in the *South Australian Register* on 19 December 1840:

> Died. Of brain fever, yesterday morning, after a few days' illness, Mr James Bell, of the South Australian Company's Commercial Office, and late of Drysdale[18], Dumfriesshire, deeply regretted by all who knew him.

All his hopes had ended there, his plans for a new life, and his dreams for his 'C.P.'. The 23-year-old was buried at West Terrace Cemetery; perhaps William Elphick and Alexander McLean were there, with new friends from the store and the Scots Church, as the Reverend Drummond read the burial service over the grave. And so ended the life of the man we have come to know so well in the pages of his journal.

Except it did not quite finish there, at the end of 1840, in the parched ground of the city's cemetery. Because

---

17 Gouger Street Presbyterian Church, minutes of managers' meetings, 6 October 1840, p. 9 (SRG 123/6/1).

18 This was incorrect: his birthplace was Dryfesdale.

someone went through James's papers after his death. And that someone presumably wrote to his brother Charles in Peelhouses. And presumably 'C.P.' also heard the news, months after the event—or maybe she already knew it in her heart of hearts, in that typical Scots way. Whatever the case, James Bell's diary, written for 'C.P.', made its way back across the sea according to the original plan, and was treasured for the lifetime, at least, of she for whom it was written. And it survived beyond her lifetime, and the lives of all who knew James, or were related to him, and somehow it was not destroyed. In a new century and millennium it resurfaced from obscurity on a bookstall at an English market, and was bought at auction by the State Library of South Australia. How it came to be on the bookstall is another story, yet to be told.

PLANTER 1839
PASSENGER AND
CREW LIST

Cabin passengers:

ALEXANDER, Samuel and Rebecca and child, of Ipswich,
England

DUDDELL, G.

HARRIS, S.

HOLMES, Captain John William

NIAS, Joseph Somerset

NICHOLSON, Arthur Bolt and Margaret, and two children,
including Ann Jane born at sea

NICHOLSON, Robert

RICHARDSON

Intermediate passengers:

BELL, James, of Dryfesdale, Dumfriesshire, Scotland

ELPHICK, William Kennard and Susanna (nee Elliot)

Steerage passengers:

BLACKEBY, Hannah, 25, seamstress, Stamford Hill, London

BURGESS, Henry, 17, labourer of Charing Kent; agent: George Whiting

CAMAC, John, 32, and Catherine (nee Reed), 30, and son (John), shepherd late agricultural labourer, Bermondsey

CANHAM, John, 38, and Mary Anne, 36, currier and boot-maker, St Leonards, Shoreditch, and four children (John, Charles, Margaret and unknown); agent: Supt of Emigration

CLARK, Catherine J., 15, servant, 17 Queen Street, Leith, Scotland; agent: Messrs Adamson and Co.

CROSBY, Daniel, 27, Beckingham, Lincolnshire

DOE, Leamon, 18, cabinetmaker, Bramforth, Suffolk

DURIEU, Henry Joseph, 43, and Lucy (nee Taylor), 38, carpenter and gunsmith, 21 Fuller Street, Bethnal Green, and three sons and four daughters including:

   DURIEU, Emma, 18, seamstress, 21 Fuller Street, Bethnal Green

   DURIEU, Catherine, 15, seamstress, 21 Fuller Street, Bethnal Green

   (Also younger children: Lucy, Henry, William, Ellen, Charles)

FIVEASH, Robert Archibald

FORDER, Henry, 24, and wife, 20, shoemaker, Amesbury, Wiltshire; agent: Rev. J.H. Alt

GOODWIN, John, 24, and Sarah (nee Blackeby), 22, and son
  (Jesse), shepherd, Kingsland, Hereford

HARRIS, Robert, 18, domestic servant, Ipswich; agent:
  J. Alexander

HAY, Alexander, 18, warper and packer, Newson, Dumferm-
  line, Scotland; agent: E.H. Mears

HIGGINS, Daniel, 22, of Buckinghamshire

HIGGINS, James, 26 (brother to Daniel)

INNIS, William, 27, farm servant, Wapping; agent: Nicholson

JAMES, William

KEANE, Honora, 26, dressmaker, Bethnal Green

KEMP, William, 25, and Mary Ann (nee Carnell), 23, labourer,
  Rowe, Devonshire; agent: Captain Holmes

KERRY, William

KIDDIE

LUCAS, Maria, 23, domestic servant, Hockstead, Suffolk; agent:
  Samuel Alexander

MACGOWAN, James, 51, and Susan (nee Jackson), 44, schoolmaster and brewer, Seacombe, Liverpool; agent: J. Hurry;
  two sons and nine daughters including:

  MACGOWAN, Susan, 18, seamstress and teacher, Seacombe,
    Liverpool

  MACGOWAN, Agnes, 16, seamstress and teacher, 31 Seymour
    Street, Liverpool

  MACGOWAN, Mary Ann, 15, seamstress and confectioner,
    Park Road, Liverpool

  (Also younger children: Elizabeth, Anne, Helen, James,
    Mary, Jean, Jessie and John)

MCLEAN, Alexander, 34, and Mary (nee McAllum), 33, and three sons (Hugh, Allan, Gilbert), shepherd, Achnacree, Argyle, Scotland

MERRETT, Ann, 24, domestic servant, Newenham, Devon; agent: Captain Holmes

MERRETT, Charles, 20, gardener and rope maker, Newenham, Devon; agent: Captain Holmes

MORRIS, George, 29, and Elizabeth (nee Dawson), 27, gardener, and son (George), St Sedwell, Exeter; agent: Captain Holmes

MUGG, Thomas, 44, and Mary Ann (nee Sanders), 44, and five children (Selina, Elizabeth, Hannah, William, George), cabinetmaker, 23 Ernest Street, Regent's Park, London

MUGG, James, 17, labourer, 23 Ernest Street, Regent's Park, London

MUGG, Thomas junior, 15, cabinetmaker, 23 Ernest Street, Regent's Park, London

PERRY, John, 49, widower, and three children (John, Harriet and Susan), Speldhurst, Kent; agent: George Whiting

PERRY, Sarah, 21, domestic servant, Tonbridge, Wiltshire; agent: George Whiting

PERRY, Charlotte, 18, domestic servant, Speldhurst, Kent; agent: George Whiting

PERRY, Sophia, 15, domestic servant, Tonbridge, Wiltshire; agent: George Whiting

SMITH, Eliza, 26, domestic servant, Greenwich; agent: E.H. Mears

STENNETT

STHELIN, Henry

STRONG, Caroline, 19, farm servant, Enford, Wiltshire; agent: Rev. J.H. Alt

TAYLOR, David, 29, and wife, 28, labourer, Austonley, Holmfirth, Yorkshire; agent: H. Hughlings

TAYLOR, Elizabeth, 29, domestic servant, Greenwich; agent: E.H. Mears

TAYLOR, Mary, 56?, widow, tailor and staymaker, 21 Fuller Street, Bethnal Green, mother of Lucy Durieu

TOWNSEND, John, 28, and Grace, 27, of Ide, Devon, and three daughters (Emma, Elizabeth and Mary); agent: Captain Holmes

WILKIN, John, 27, and Hannah (nee Smith), 29, agricultural labourer, Burstall, Suffolk, and two children (Alfred and Emma—both died before embarkation), agent: J. Alexander

Crew:

BEAZLEY, Thomas (Captain)
MUSTART, G. (First Officer)
SHAW, W. (Second Officer)
WITHERICK, William (Third Officer)—remained in South Australia
MCDONALD, carpenter
PHILLIPS, J., seaman
MCINTYRE, J.
FIDDLER, J.
TAYLOR, G.
BICKLY, Joseph
BEALE, Dan

FIELD, Richard
BLAKE, Thomas
7 LASCARS

Note: This list is based on the brief manifest of the *Planter*, together with details of individual applications for assisted passages. Further details have been extracted from a number of sources in the State Library of South Australia, including South Australian Births, Deaths and Marriages, the registers of Holy Trinity Anglican Church Adelaide, the 1841 Census, and issues of South Australian newspapers on the Trove website.

BIBLIOGRAPHY

Published

Colwell, Max, *Ships and Seafarers in Australian Waters*, Lansdowne, Melbourne, 1973.

Hay, Agnes Grant, *Footprints: A memoir of the late Alexander Hay*, Elliot Stock, London, 1899.

Hetherington, R., 'Gawler, George (1795–1869)', *Australian Dictionary of Biography*, Melbourne University Press, Melbourne, 1966–.

Hope, Penelope, *The Voyage of the Africaine*, Heinemann Educational, South Yarra, 1968.

Kerr, Colin, *A Excelent Coliney: The practical idealists of 1836–1846*, Rigby, Adelaide, 1978.

Laube, Anthony, *A Lady at Sea: The adventures of Agnes Grant Hay*, Glenelg, A. Laube, 2001.

Morgan, Dalma and Poole, Harry, *Voyage of a Lifetime,* Brighton SA, D. Morgan and H. Poole, 1978.

Moore, Bryce, Garwood, Helen and Lutton, Nancy, *The Voyage Out: 100 years of sea travel to Australia*, Fremantle Arts Centre Press, South Fremantle, 1991.

Norman, W.A., *History of the City of Mitcham*, City of Mitcham, Mitcham, 1953.

Parsons, Ronald, *Southern Passages: A maritime history of South Australia*, Wakefield Press, Netley SA, 1986.

Pike, Douglas, *A Paradise of Dissent*, Longmans Green & Co., London, 1957.

Sexton, R.T., *Shipping Arrivals and Departures South Australia 1627–1850*, Gould Books, Ridgehaven, 1990.

Newspapers

South Australian Register 1839–1840

South Australian 1839–1840

Unpublished

Index to register of emigrant labourers applying for a free passage to South Australia 1836–1841 (State Library of South Australia, source 1529).

Copies of letters to the officers of the Colonization Commissioners for South Australia 1836–1840 (State Records of South Australia, GRG 48/5/1).

Gouger Street Presbyterian Church, managers' meetings 1839–1851 (State Library of South Australia, SRG 123/6/1).

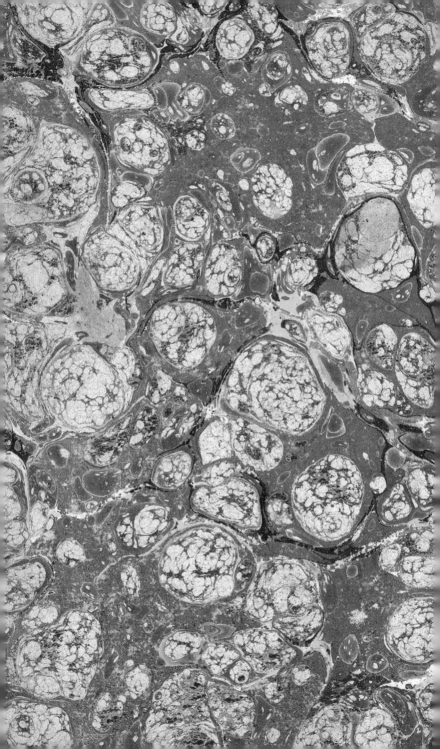